STANLEY MORISON DISPLAYED

STANLEY MORISON DISPLAYED

AN EXAMINATION OF HIS EARLY

TYPOGRAPHIC WORK

BY

HERBERT JONES

Foreword by Sir William Emrys Williams, CBE DLitt.

LONDON

FREDERICK MULLER LIMITED

1976

First published in Great Britain in 1976 by
Frederick Muller Limited, London, NW2 6LE

Printed and bound by
W & J Mackay Limited, Chatham

ISBN: 0 584 10352 2

FOR E.V.

ACKNOWLEDGEMENTS

First of all I am indebted to James Moran for constant advice and encouragement in writing this book and in various and invaluable ways to Rowley Atterbury, Nicolas Barker, George Bull, T. F. Burns, William Clowes, Brooke Crutchley, Kenneth Day, Miss Livia Gollancz, Lionel Gray, Ernest Ingham, Alan Jones, James Mosley, Mrs. M. C. Sidgwick and Sir William Emrys Williams; and to the following for permission to reproduce their copyright material: The Society of Authors on behalf of the Bernard Shaw Estate, B. T. Batsford Ltd., The Bodley Head Ltd., The British Academy, The British Council, The British Library Board, Jonathan Cape Ltd., Cambridge University Press, Victor Gollancz Ltd., Lund Humphries Publishers Ltd., Macmillan London and Basingstoke, The Medici Society of London, The Monotype Corporation Ltd., and to the Oxford University Press, Oxford, for permission to quote from The Poetical Works of Robert Bridges.

CONTENTS

LIST OF ILLUSTRATIONS

FOREWORD

by Sir William Emrys Williams

Typography is one of the most fascinating, almost hypnotic, of the applied arts, and those who practise it do so with uncommon fervour and dedication. The doyen of typographers in this century was Stanley Morison and this perceptive study of his work is written by a craftsman of comparable quality. Unlike some of his famous predecessors in printing, such as Caxton and William Morris, who were well into their middle age (Caxton was past sixty) when they entered the trade, Stanley Morison applied himself to it when still a young man, with all the advantages that youth commands in the pursuit of creative enterprises.

Gifted and uncompromising, Morison was one of the main driving forces of the revitalising period in the development of typography immediately following the First World War. He reaffirmed the fundamentals of bookwork with force and precision, asserting the importance of the appearance of the page whether it was of a leaflet or a book, magazine or newspaper, all aimed at changing our bad habit of looking so casually at what we read, and helping to establish a link between the printer and the public that never existed before. He practised what he preached, not in any academic retreat but in the hard commercial world. Never an ordinary employee he chose his collaborators always with an eye to exposing some new capability of printing. He cooperated, for example, with the poet Robert Bridges to show how printing and language could be fused to perfection. A different, but equally significant, partnership was that with the publisher Victor Gollancz, which resulted in a new style of bookjacket with an abrasive typography in the service of publicity.

Morison was a controversial figure and some of his work and claims are still open to question. Discussion continues among typographical and palaeographical specialists as to the extent of his achievement, but he was undoubtedly a major influence in both the typographical revival of the nineteen twenties and in the awakening of interest in typographical history. What Herbert Jones has done so well is to draw attention to, as it were, Morison unalloyed—his title *Stanley Morison Displayed* is particularly apt. By showing and discussing much of Morison's actual and early work (not without a degree of

11

criticism) he has provided a valuable aid to students of typography who are concerned with forming their own judgement about Morison's contribution to printing. For these reasons I cordially recommend this memorable revelation of the work of Stanley Morison both to those who have forgotten and to a new generation that wants, indeed needs, to know about him.

STANLEY MORISON DISPLAYED

1

AN INTRODUCTION TO TYPOGRAPHY

The first time the world, or rather that small, interested part of it, saw the name of Stanley Morison displayed in print was in 1913 on the cover of the crusading graphic arts periodical *The Imprint*, as author of an article about liturgical books. There was little to indicate that in the following decade he would be described as standing at the head of writers about printing or that when he died some half a century later public tribute would be paid to him as "one of the most influential Englishmen of his generation."[1]

The limited purpose of this book is to show Stanley Morison as a practical typographer—that is, as a person responsible for the arrangement of type and the appearance of printed matter.

Much of the material selected relates to the nineteen-twenties, the decisive period when the work he did was most varied in character, the period in which he rose from being a lay-amateur (his own phrase) to an accomplished professional. In those few years he developed an impeccable taste in typography and considerable invention, one of the essentials in any art, in his use of typographic material. To appreciate fully his typography it is necessary to look at it life-size, and in detail, to dissect it where it would be instructive to do so and this has been attempted.

That Morison was much more than a typographer has long been conceded and it has been underlined since his death not only by the spate of obituaries due to a prominent man of letters but also by important publications concerning his life and work and by other manifestations of esteem; the exhibition arranged by the British Museum authorities and presented appropriately in the King's Library was perhaps the most impressive of these.

It is a ritual for writers about typography today to refer to the "revival of printing" at the end of the nineteenth century. To the layman, the non-printer, this is a misleading term, with its implication that there had been a decline in the actual practice of printing at that time. This could not be further from the truth for the trade generally was going through a period of expansion. What is meant by the term "revival of printing" is the revival at the end of the nineteenth century of interest in the better printing of books in general, and it is in this context that it is accurate to speak of a decline, a

[1] *Stanley Morison: a portrait.* The Trustees of the British Museum. 1971.

15

decline in standards of taste, materials and execution. To be more specific, design was a negligible factor, type faces had become emasculated, the temptation to use the lower grades of paper that were available was less often resisted, and presswork—that is, the inking of the type and its impression on the paper—fell to a low standard.

However, it is important to remember that the decline was not as great as is sometimes suggested, and it is worth while to consider briefly the developments in printing during the hundred years in question. Some authorities point to the falling off in patronage at the beginning of the century as one of the factors affecting the standards of bookwork; others to the depression of trade following the Napoleonic wars and others to the technological advances such as the cylindrical printing machine which required a technique different to that of the historic hand-press and yet to be learned. The separation of printing and publishing was perhaps a more profound cause and this is the view that Morison himself supported. The growth of new forms of commercial printing brought to the trade workmen who had neither the skills nor understanding possessed by those who had been trained in bookwork.

As interesting as this line of enquiry could be if carried further, the fact is that many book printers continued to turn out work of high quality all through the nineteenth century. As well as printers themselves being aware of their better traditions, there were those among their customers who had an understanding of aesthetics and were concerned in getting the best possible results in their work. This point could not be made clearer than by a letter written by Sir Francis Chantry, President of the Royal Academy, in 1824, to John Murray the publisher of Byron, asking him if Clowes "is a respectable tradesman and a printer of sufficient importance to be entrusted with the printing of so important a specimen of typography as the Royal Academy Catalogue."[1]

There was, inside and outside the trade, a developing interest in the artistic requirements of printing. The Great Exhibition of 1851 was one obvious example of official encouragement of that desirable trend which, in turn, led to the full growth of the arts and crafts movement from which stemmed all the ideas that animated the "revival of printing" (which Morison described as the "romantic discovery by artists of its appeal as a handicraft"[2]), and which indeed helped to create the climate in which a person like him could flourish. It is an interesting coincidence that in the very year that Morison was born, a group of people including Andrew Tuer, Robert Hilton, Raithby Lawrence and George W. Jones founded the *British Printer*; in that year also classes in

---

[1] *Family Business 1803–1953*. W. B. Clowes (William Clowes).
[2] *The Art of Printing*. Lecture to British Academy. Note to illustrations.

typography were started in Edinburgh and London aimed at improving the standards of printing generally.

One of the most remarkable of Morison's gifts was the speed in which he accumulated his knowledge of printing, all the more remarkable because his choice of calling was completely fortuitous, not encouraged by any previous craft or artistic training. Later in life he was sometimes less than kind to his mentors and rarely revealed the origins of typographical ideas, but this does not detract from the fact that he became the major influence in the typographical revival of the nineteen-twenties. His first acquaintance with books was made as a boy with an avid appetite for general literature but it was a chance reading about the technical aspects of printing that quickened his interest. Then the sight of classical bookwork in the British Museum gave it reality.

Was it instinct, poverty or curiosity that sent Morison there at an impressionable age? We shall never know, but we can be sure it was not the deadly sin of boredom for he was, fortunately for us, a restless searcher all through his long and active life. Nowadays more people visit the British Museum in a single week than went there in a whole year at the beginning of this century, but any one of the millions who walk through its stately galleries can see the same early products of the printing press (some of them in the same display cases), which fascinated Morison so long ago.

Any study of typography must have some grasp of its history, and there is no better place to start—just as Morison did—than in the King's Library. Standing at the head of the Museum's permanent exhibition of printed books is the earliest German work exemplified in the Bibles of Gutenberg and Fust and Schoeffer. From Germany the visitor moves to Italy where he sees, almost side by side, two editions of Cicero unforgettable in their elegance of form. Both were printed in Venice at the end of the fifteenth century, one by Joannes de Spira, the other by the renowned Nicolas Jenson of whose roman type his partners wrote in an advertisement in 1482, two years after his death: "the characters are so intelligently and carefully elaborated that the letters are neither smaller, larger nor thicker than reason or pleasure demand," an analysis that burned into Morison's memory for it expressed perfectly his attitude to letter design in later years. The exhibition continues in chronological order, showing the work of the great printers of Europe up to the twentieth century with such magnificent volumes that moved Morison to say "it would seem almost a liberty to read and a blasphemy to hold on your knees."[1] A few steps from the King's Library are the manuscript books, another of his passions, and then across the main hall where, acknowledging his affection for the

[1] *On Type Faces*, Stanley Morison, The Medici Society, 1923.

BM, Morison recalls: "I first set eyes on the Rosetta stone and began to wonder why the several branches of the human family wrote in the funny ways they did."[1]

Morison was also beginning his own collection of books, an example to be followed by anyone who wishes to improve his knowledge of typography. London before the First World War was a storehouse of secondhand books offering an opportunity to anyone to build a library on almost any subject; it still is, only the price has changed.

So, while he was still in his 'teens, Morison's intellectual interests had very firmly turned to types and books and everything concerned with them. However, his chance to make closer ties with printing was delayed until, at the age of 24, he went to work as a clerk for The Westminster Press, whose offices were in the Covent Garden area with a printing works off the Harrow Road in the borough of Paddington.

More important to Morison than the convenience of transport was the declared intention of the firm to produce a magazine to be called *The Imprint*. When he read the prospectus he felt that at last he was getting closer to his inner desires. It reads as fresh and honest as it did when it was written in 1912:

> *The Imprint* will be an illustrated monthly magazine, price one shilling net, devoted to the printing and allied trades. It will deal with book and periodical printing, tracts, catalogues, circulars, posters and other forms of printed matter; typographic printing and type-founding; stereotyping; wood-engraving, process-block making, and electrotyping; lithography and metalography; offset and collotype; intaglio printing, including etching and engraving; machinery, bookbinding; penmanship, palaeography and illuminating; black and white drawing for reproduction.
>
> 'The Imprint* will appeal to master printers and binders, and workers in every branch of the trade; to the makers of machinery, paper, blocks, ink, type, rollers, etc., and to all those dealing in printer's supplies, to the publishing trade in general, and to the advertising and printing managers in all large establishments; it will also make a special appeal to students specialising in the graphic arts. . . . The aim of *The Imprint* is to benefit the printing and allied trades, to afford a friendly medium of intercommunication, and to show the place for craftsmanship in the printing trade.
>
> 'The Imprint* will endeavour in this connection to bring into the closest relation possible, the artist, the author, and the craftsman; and, where possible, to merge their identity; in a word, to make an artist of the crafts-

---

[1] In a speech of thanks for the award of the Bibliographical Society's Gold Medal, March, 1948.

man and a craftsman of the artist. The education of the apprentice and the art student will be treated with the consideration which this important matter demands.

Fighting words.

The Imprint was a landmark in printing and "the influence it exerted on typographical design has still to be fully evaluated" was the judgement made in a commemorative issue of *The Monotype Newsletter* fifty years later. The trade press of the day was, to say the least, dull, and *The Imprint*, though a commercial failure was an artistic success, and it was the spiritual parent of the more glamorous *Fleuron* and other journals which appeared years later. It was also a turning point for Morison, and although the magazine and his connection with it lasted less than a year he had as a result gained an insight into publishing, made his first step into authorship, and above all improved his theoretical knowledge of typography against the time when he would apply it so zealously and so effectively.

2

THE PRINTER'S RESOURCES

The most enjoyable as well as the most responsible task that falls to the typographer who works for a printer is the designing of a specimen showing off the firm's typographic resources. On the several occasions that Morison had this job to do he showed characteristic inventiveness, giving each project a different impact. The first was the now celebrated broadsheet for the Pelican Press in 1921. The format was not new to printing, for one of the best known paintings related to the trade is the portrait of William Caslon, in the pose of a Greek senator, holding a copy of the 1734 specimen of his types. But the Pelican broadsheet, a joint production of Francis Meynell and Morison, was a gargantuan affair measuring 40 inches by 30 inches (quad crown) four or more times the size of Caslon's, and it just could not be ignored. In 1918, before Morison joined Pelican, Meynell had produced a smaller broadsheet showing the types held by the Press.

From a purely technical point of view the production of such a formidable sheet presented problems to the compositors and machine minders. In imposing the inside forme of the sheet there was no possibility of using the long bar or one of the short bars in the chase, making it difficult to get a satisfactory lock up. Also, the total weight of the type metal, a hundredweight or so, made lifting the forme off the imposing stone and carrying it downstairs to the machine room a hazardous undertaking. Furthermore, such a large forme of type tends to be "springy," a condition notorious for making perfect inking and printing harder to achieve. These parts of the drama of printing are, as it were, played off-stage.

In terms of content the selection though comparatively small was choice; "very fit and very few" is how the types were described in number two of the Pelican's information sheet, *A Printer's Miscellany*. Caslon Old Face and Cloister were the strongest series, ranging from six to seventy-two point; ten sizes of the recently arrived Kennerley and eight sizes of another Goudy letter, the Forum capitals; seven sizes of Nicolas Cochin and a few sizes of two charming ornamented types, Moreau-le-jeune and Fournier-le-jeune, and finally there were five sizes of the Shank's Caxton, the black letter for which Morison had a special liking. "First used in England by the Pelican" is a claim proudly made about several of them. And of course there were the faces for machine composition: Italian, Old Face, Imprint, Plantin and Old Style, "and these faces have been improved by the addition and substitution of special letters and ligatures designed on the order of the Pelican Press." What further added to its attraction was the wealth and distinctiveness of ornaments, initials and borders from historical sources and this, together with the exuberant display and a catching enthusiasm in its language, amounted to an affirmation, or reaffirmation if you like, of a belief or pride in printing. "The Pelican Press" it said,

> is not prepared to do work at the lowest market quality. Its aim is not merely to see how cheaply, but also how *well* (within strictly appropriate limits of costs), any job can be done. Yet the prices at the Pelican Press are often lower than those of the small company of printers who still maintain a tradition and a style: & sometimes lower than those who know neither style nor tradition & who substitute for them an excessive use of expensive processes.

The whole thing was vastly different from the general run of trade salesmanship and it had many admirers. Frank Sidgwick, the publisher, was one of the first to see it and immediately wrote to express his appreciation which Morison said was "sweet music to my ears," indicating that he evidently regarded it as one of his productions. Some years later Sidgwick wrote in an article in *The Fleuron*, No. 3: "I well remember the pleasure with which I beheld . . . the large display poster of the Pelican Press founts."

Admire it Sidgwick certainly did, but he never used it. Instead he carefully put it back in its envelope and stored it away with his other specimens of printing so that fifty years later it was in fine condition as can be seen from the photographs reproduced.

It had its faults. The principal one being that it could not readily be put to practical use. For example, if it is placed on a wall, at what height should it be hung? If low enough for the small sizes at the top of the column to be read, then one would have to be bent double or on one's knees to consult the larger sizes lower down. Then, what happens when one wants to refer to the material on the other side? If it were not hung on a wall but kept in the folded state, to be opened out whenever it was needed for reference, it would not be long before it was in shreds.

What the working typographer demands of a type specimen is nothing less than the showing of every letter of every size of type available including all the additional sorts from figures and commercial signs to punctuation marks. And a substantial amount of solid and leaded matter of sizes available for machine setting. The main reason for this is simply that it is essential for

(1) The 1921 Pelican Press specimen sheet was sent out in a magnificent envelope which together with the rich Ratdolt border printed in black and red lettering created a sense of anticipation.

accurate casting off. The extract from the Pelican specimen sheet of two sizes of Caslon Old Face, 6-point and 72-point, shows how inadequate this tiny amount is for the typographer's purpose.

The showing of every size of type was taken for granted when there were fewer faces. It would be almost impossible for a typefounder or a printer to accomplish this within the confines of a single manageable book today. The loose-leaf binder is a practical system but it lacks the attractiveness of a bound

(2) When it was opened out to its full quad crown size the specimen was impressive; it was frustrating in use because of the limited amount of each size of type shown, with the additional problem of how to refer to the matter on the other side of the sheet.

book and there is the unavoidable hazard of loss or mutilation. To show the amount of material available at Pelican adequately would have necessitated a quarto book running to sixty pages or more and presumably this was beyond the company's financial resources.

It was inevitable that some adverse comment would be passed on their specimen, and Pelican did not hesitate to print one of the more crude outbursts, which it called a case of "hardened ignorance." This appeared in the

booklet *The Craft of Printing*, reporting that the head of the publicity department of a world-famous London house refused to accept the Pelican broadsheet on the ground that he had a hundredweight of "that sort of stuff" sent
to him every week. Who ever wrote that criticism was more than ignorant.
Apart from its bad manners it was not true. In 1921 the display types in
printer's cases were still largely of nineteenth-century origin: Latins of all
kinds (expanded, elongated, bold), Windsor, Chatsworth and endless ornamented faces. The fact that some of these types have been unearthed in recent

15 ABCDE
abcdf 72 pt

TYPE NUMBER ONE - ABCDEFGHIJKLMNOPQQURSTUVWXYZÆŒ&ABCDEFGHIJKLMNOPQRSTUVWXYZÆŒabcdefghijklmnop
qrstuvwxyzæœfiflfffffifflstfhffifflb12345£*ABCDEFGHIJKLMNOPQQURSTUVWXYZ&abcdefghijklmnopqrstuvwxyzæœ* Old face six point

(3) A few letters of the larger sizes did little justice to the character of the
letter; at the other end of the scale one line of 6 point did not provide a
proper base for calculation.

years for use in advertisements does not make them beautiful. It proves merely
that fashion is not only fickle but freakish, whereas great style endures without interruption. There were many sans serifs, most of the condensed variety,
and were known as gothic, doric or grotesque but seldom as sans serif. When
it came to spelling there was no general agreement as to whether it was serif,
serriff or surruph which as Morison pointed out suggested an aural tradition.[1]
Cheltenham was the most popular face of the day; the types of Frederic
Goudy had not yet attained the wide use in England that they did a few years
later.

However a revolution was in progress and its achievements were clearly
demonstrated when in 1930 the Saint Bride Institute put on an exhibition of
the type specimens in its collection, the catalogue listing 698 specimens, with

[1] *Politics and Scripts*, (Oxford University Press).

more than 300 named faces, issued between 1918 and 1930 by 34 typefounders and their agents. If the critic of the Pelican Press broadsheet had waited ten years to make his comment there could have been some substance for his complaint. For as quickly as the typefounders produced new faces the printers in turn saw this new material as a means of attracting work and got out their own specimen books to show them off. The production of printer's type specimen books expanded enormously and what was a trickle in 1921 became a flood by the end of the decade.

Finally, an anecdote about the Pelican broadsheet. Although it says on the splendidly decorated envelope "By letter post from the Pelican Press", the distinguished package was in fact delivered by hand to Sidgwick's office in the Adelphi. According to Stacey, the firm's looker-out, packer and general odd-job man and master of cockney semantics, it was handed in at No. 3 Adam Street by "a long geezer with a black titfer." Morison to a tee. From which we can deduce two things: that he was anxious that a copy of the specimen got to Sidgwick safely and without delay, and that at that time he had no false pride about acting as a messenger.

The criticisms made of the Pelican Press broadsheet cannot be levelled against the magnificent specimens Morison produced for the Cloister Press. The plan here was a portfolio of loose four-page french-fold sheets and again the size is impressive: 15 inches by 10 inches (crown folio). This gives the opportunity for luxurious display, especially of larger sizes, as can be seen in the reproduction of the Forum capitals and the English Black Letter.

Least successful of the Cloister specimens was the Garamond. "Not very satisfactory" wrote Morison to D. B. Updike.[1] and it is easy to see the reasons for his disappointment. The title page in particular lacks form and cohesion. The matter on pages two and three is unevenly set and badly spaced. The repetition of the two sizes, 48 point and 36 point italic at the bottom of page three serves no purpose except that of showing the complete capital and lower case alphabets. The fourth page, showing text setting of roman and italic versions of five sizes, is well arranged as regards the disposition of the areas of type matter but, unusual for Morison, we do not grasp instantly and clearly what is being shown. To take a simple case, the half dozen lines of 6-point roman and italic are almost hidden beneath the four and a half inches of 8-point matter pressing down on them with hardly a breathing space separating them. The side references used to identify the size, as on pages two and three, would have been helpful here also. Morison must have been nodding.

In 1923 *On Type Faces* appeared, oddly described on the title page as containing "examples of the use of type for the printing of books," but what

[1] *Stanley Morison*, Nicolas Barker, (Macmillan).

THIRTY-SIX POINT

A B C D E F G H I
J
K
L 1 2 3 4 5 6 7 8 9 0
M N O P Q R S T
U
V
W

THESE LETTERS ARE
BASED UPON THE STONE
INSCRIPTIONS OF CLASS

ICAL ROME · 30 POINT I

TYPE INCLUDES
CAPITALS & FIG
URES ONLY. THE
LETTER FINDS
ITS BEST USE IN
HEADINGS AND
TITLINGS, ALSO

INITIAL LETTERS.
IT POSSESSES WEIGHT
AS WELL AS GRACE

MINUSCULES OR
LOWER CASE
FORMS WERE
NOT EVOLVED
UNTIL THE SIXTH
OR SEVENTH
CENT. A.D. FORUM

FORUM PERSONALITY
FITS IT FOR NEWSPA
PER ADVERTISING · 18

THE CLOISTER PRESS · HEATON MERSEY · NR. MANCHESTER

(4) Morison had a special liking for Goudy's capitals and this page from the Cloister Press specimen displays the short range of sizes of Forum effectively. In the original the first and fifth lines and the letters connecting them at left and right and the row of numerals were printed in blue. (Actual size)

Statutes relating to the Poor

The general Statutes which treat concerning Labourers, poor People, and some other People, who wilfully become chargeable to a Common-wealth, (and therefore ought properly to be distinguish'd by another Name,) are, viz.

¶ i. Stat. 5 Eliz. Cap. 4. Concerning Labourers, Artificers, Servants, and Apprentices, ; with 1 Jac. 3, 6, for raising the Wages of Labourers, and other Artificers

¶ ii. More particularly relating to poor People ; as 43 Eliz. 2. 1 Jac. 1. 25. 7 Jac. 1. cap. 3. 3 Car. 1. cap. 4. 13 & 14 Car. 2. cap. 12. 22 & 23 Car. 2. cap. 8. Stat. 1 Jac. 2. cap. 17

¶ iii. Such as concern Bastards, lewd Women, Vagabonds, Vagrants, Rogues, Beggars, &c. as 18 Eliz. cap. 3. 39 Eliz. 1. 4. Stat. 39 Eliz. 1. 17. Stat 1 Jac. 1. 1. 7. Stat. 7 Jac. 1 cap 4

Artificers, Workmen, and Labourers, that conspire together concerning their Work or Wages, every of them so conspiring shall forfeit for the First Offence 10l. to the KING; and if he pay it not within Six Days after Conviction, by Witness, Confession, or otherwise, he shall suffer Twenty Days Imprisonment, and during that Time shall have no Sustenance but Bread and Water :

2 & 3 Eliz. 6. c. 15. Artificers Workmen & Labourers

¶ For the Second Offence he shall forfeit 20l. and that not paid within Six Days, as aforesaid, shall suffer the Pillory :

¶ And for the Third Offence he shall forfeit 40l. and that not paid within the said time, shall again suffer the Pillory, lose one of his Ears, and be ever after taken as a Man infamous, and not to be credited.

English Black, 10, 12, 18, and 24 pt

◄ A SPECIMEN OF THE GARAMOND TYPE ►

TEN SIZES SIX TO FORTY-EIGHT POINT ROMAN
AND A COMPANION ITALIC

first cut by CLAUDE GARAMOND in 1535 for king FRANCIS the FIRST of FRANCE and now revived in English printing at the CLOISTER PRESS PARRS WOOD LANE HEATON MERSEY near MANCHESTER in the year of our Lord MCMXXI

(5) The Cloister Press specimen of Old Caslon Black-letter which it recommended when an "old style" effect was desired.
(6) For the Garamond it was claimed that it was now "revived in English printing at the Cloister Press". (Originals 15 ins. by 10 ins.)

it really is, of course, is a type specimen book, with a difference. It beautifully displays twenty-four types, some of classical origin and others of contemporary design. Morison takes each of the twenty-four faces and sets out every one in a different and ingenious manner in what can truthfully be described as a *tour de force*. To Frank Sidgwick this was what a type specimen book should be and it was the one he most frequently used in his work. To show how he thought it could be improved he took the copy Morison presented to him and cut off the fore-edge margins so that he could thumb index the contents at the opening page of each design. The state of this index shows the wear and tear of regular use. For an example of how to profit by experience, compare the layout of the smaller sizes of the Cloister in "On Type Faces" with that for the similar range of sizes of Garamond in Morison's Cloister specimen.

The two centre pages from the Cloister Press Garamond specimen:

The GARAMOND LETTER
THE FIRST PRINTING
in France was produced in
THE YEAR 1470 BY THREE
German Craftsmen. They used
A ROMAN LETTER FOR
their first Book, an edition of
LIBER EPISTVLARVM
by Gaspar of Barizzia, a noted
ITALIAN SCHOLAR OF THE
Renaissance. They were in advance
OF THEIR TIME, HOWEVER, AS
the black letter was firmly rooted in public
ESTEEM. FOR THE FOLLOWING
fifty years French printers used the gothic
TYPE. IN KING FRANCIS THE FIRST
however, the Craft found an enlightened patron

THIS MONARCH INSTITUTED AN OFFICIAL
State Printing House, and circa 1535 appointed
CLAUDE GARAMOND HIS ROYAL PRINTER
This famous designer and typographer, who was a pupil of
THE RENOWNED GEOFROY TORY, HAD BEEN A
goldsmith's engraver. Garamond's first notable success as a Type
CUTTER WAS A GREEK FOUNT. THEN HE CUT THE
magnificent roman and its beautiful italic here shown. These types were
AN UNQUALIFIED SUCCESS, AND *CLOISTER PRESS IS VERY PLEASED TO*
as they were very widely imitated Claude *announce its possession of the recut Garamond*
GARAMOND'S INFLUENCE UPON OLD *LETTER IN TEN SIZES WHICH IT*
face letter forms was remarkable. The Dutch & *commends to those of its customers who desire to have*
OTHER FOUNDERS, AND EVEN OUR OWN *ANNOUNCEMENTS, BOOKS, ETC, PRINTED IN A*
William Caslon, never surpassed the elegance and *type of remarkable grace and spirit.*
INTEREST OF THE LETTER CUT BY THE FRENCH *ABCDEFGHIJKLMNOPQRSTUVWXYZ ABC*
royal printer. The degradation of printing during the 18th
AND 19th CENTURIES LED TO THE ALMOST COMPLETE
abandonment of all old face types, including the Garamond. The Cloister

ABCDEFGHIJLMNOPQ
RSTUVWXYZabcdefghijk
lmnopqrstuvwxyz &

ABCDEFGHIJKLMNOPQRSTUV
WXYZ abcdefghijklmnopqrstuvvwuxyz

fr ffl ffi fi fl sp tt ll us ct is as st 1234567890 1234567890

(7) The two centre pages from the Cloister Press Garamond specimen which Morison said was not very satisfactory probably because it was one of the first to be done (1921) but it is notable for the quality and continuity of the wording which he supplied and which became a fascinating feature of most of his type specimens. (Original 15 ins. by 10 ins.)

The layout of the smaller sizes of Caslon and Kennerley show the care he took to make attractive variations for the reader. At the foot of the Caslon page Frank Sidgwick wrote: "10 pt.—one of the best—omitted." One can only wonder how it happened. However, Morison must have been glad to see the back of this particular undertaking for it involved a lot of detailed work in writing, layout and organisation in getting the material together which was left to him to do. In spite of his usually methodical manner there were lapses, and one of the blanks in the prelims, probably intended to be a half title between the prelims proper and the specimens, has become instead a page of corrigenda. It states that owing to certain foreign types having to be set up and printed abroad, errors have occurred in the English spelling and lists fourteen errors.

My dear boy: Though I employ so much of my time in writing to you, I confess I have often my doubts whether it is to any purpose. I know how unwelcome advice generally is; I know that those who want it most like it and follow it least; and I know, too, that the advice of parents, more particularly, is ascribed to the moroseness, the imperiousness, or the garrulity of old-age. But then, on the other hand, I flatter myself that as your own reason (though too young as yet to suggest much to you of itself) is, however, strong enough to enable you both to judge of, and receive, plain truths: I flatter myself (I say) that your own reason, young as it is, must tell you that I can have no interest but yours in the advice I give you; and that, consequently, you will at least weigh and consider it well: in which case, some of it will, I hope, have its effect. Do not think that I mean to dictate as a parent; I only mean to advise as a friend, and an indulgent one too: and do not apprehend that I mean to check your pleasures; of which, on the contrary, I only desire to be the guide, not the censor. Let my experience supply your want of it, and clear your way, in the progress of your youth, of those thorns and briars which scratched and disfigured me in the course of mine.

I do not, therefore, so much as hint to you how absolutely dependent you are upon me; that you neither have, nor can have, a shilling in the world but from me; and I have no womanish weakness for your person. [Written October 4, 1746.]

We are too much in the habit of looking at falsehood in its darkest associations, and through the colour of its worst purposes. That indignation which we profess to feel at deceit absolute is indeed only at deceit malicious. We resent calumny, hypocrisy, and treachery because they harm us, not because they are untrue. Take the detraction and the mischief from the untruth, and we are little offended by it; turn it into praise, and we may be pleased with it. And yet it is no calumny nor treachery that do the largest sum of mischief in the world; they are continually crushed, and are felt only in being conquered. But it is the glistening and softly spoken lie; the amiable fallacy; the patriotic lie of the historian, the provident lie of the politician, the zealous lie of the partizan, the merciful lie of the friend, and the careless lie of each man to himself that cast that black mystery over humanity through which we thank any *man who pierces, as we would thank one who dug a well in a desert; happy that the thirst for truth still remains with us, even when we have wilfully left the fountains. From the " Seven Lamps."*

" The retail tradesman in especial, and even every tradesman in his station, must furnish himself with a competent stock of patience. I mean that sort of patience which is needful to bear with all sorts of impertinence, and the most provoking curiosity that it is impossible to imagine the buyers, even the worst of them, are, or can be, guilty of. A tradesman behind his counter must have no flesh and blood about him, no passions, no resentment; he must never be angry, no, not so much as seem to be so, if a customer tumbles him five hundred pounds' worth of goods, and scarce bids money for any thing; nay, though they really come to his shop with no intent to buy, as many do, only to see what is to be sold, and though he knows they cannot be better pleased than they are at some other shop where they intend to buy, 'tis all one; the tradesman must take it; he must place it to the account of his calling that 'tis his business to be ill used, and resent nothing; and so must answer as obligingly to those that give him an hour or two's trouble, and buy nothing, as he does to those who, in half the time, lay out ten or twenty pounds. The case is plain; and if some do give him trouble, and do not buy, others make amends, and do buy; and as for the trouble, 'tis the business of the shop." The short inference from this long discourse is this: that here you see how and in what manner a shopkeeper is to hold himself in the way of his business, and how that he must be a complete hypocrite if he will be a complete tradesman. The sum of the matter is this: his customers are to be his idols, he is to bow down and worship them. From the " Complete English Tradesman."

AUTOBIOGRAPHY

CHARLES LAMB

Charles Lamb, born in the Inner Temple, 10th February, 1775; educated in Christ's Hospital; afterwards a clerk in the Accountants' Office, East India House; pensioned off from that service 1825, after thirty-three years' service; is now a gentleman at large; can remember few specialities in his life worth noting, except that he once caught a swallow flying ("teste sua manu"). Below the middle stature; cast of face slightly Jewish, with no Judaic tinge in his complexional religion; stammers abominably, and is therefore more apt to discharge his occasional conversation in a quaint aphorism, or a poor quibble, than in set and edifying speeches; has consequently been libelled as a person always aiming at wit; which, as he told a dull fellow that charged him with it, is at least as good as aiming at dulness. A small eater, but not drinker; confesses a partiality for the production of the juniper-berry; was a fierce smoker of tobacco, but may be resembled to

a volcano burnt out, emitting only now and then a casual puff. Has been guilty of obtruding upon the public a tale, in prose, called "John Woodvil"; a "Farewell Ode to Tobacco," with sundry other poems, and light prose matter, collected in two slight crown octavos, and pompously christened his works, though in fact they were his recreations; and his true works may be found on the shelves of Leadenhall Street, filling some hundred folios. He is also the true Elia, whose Essays are extant in a little volume, published a year or two since, and rather better known from that name without a meaning than from any thing he has done, or can hope to do, in his own. He was also the first to draw the public attention to the old English dramatists, in a work called "Specimens of English Dramatic Writers who lived about the time of Shakspeare," published about fifteen years since. In short, all his merits and demerits to set forth would take to the end of Mr. Upcott's book, then not be told truly. He died much lamented, witness his hand, CHARLES LAMB

SONNET OF SHAKESPERE

Weary with toil, I haste me to my bed,
The dear repose for limbs with travel tired;
But then begins a journey in my head,
To work my mind, when body's work's expired:
Far then my thoughts, from far where I abide,
Intend a zealous pilgrimage to thee,
And keep my drooping eyelids open wide,
Looking on darkness which the blind do see:
Save that my soul's imaginary sight
Presents thy shadow to my sightless view,
Which, like a jewel hung in ghastly night,
Makes black night beauteous, and her old face new.
Lo, thus, by day my limbs, by night my mind,
For thee, and for myself no quiet find.

SONNET OF JOHN DONNE

*Death, be not proud, though some have called thee
Mighty and dreadful, for thou art not so:
For those whom thou think'st thou dost overthrow
Die not, poor Death; nor yet canst thou kill me.
From Rest and Sleep, which but thy picture be,
Much pleasure, then from thee much more must flow;
And soonest our best men with thee do go—
Rest of their bones and souls' delivery!
Thou'rt slave to fate, chance, kings, and desperate men,
And dost with poison, war, and sickness dwell;
And poppy our charms can make us sleep as well
And better than thy stroke. Why swell'st thou then?
One short sleep past, we wake eternally,
And Death shall be no more: Death, thou shalt die!*

Garamond 6 8 10 12 & 14 point

(8) Clarity sacrificed to symmetry in this attempt to show the roman and italic of five smaller sizes. (Reduced.)

The first press in Italy was set up at the Benedictine Monastery of Subiaco, near Rome. Some Germans were members of this community, and perhaps that was one reason why the German printers, Conrad Sweynheym and Arnold Pannartz, were welcomed by its abbot, Cardinal Turrecremata. Sweynheym, a clerk of the diocese of Mainz, was possibly one of Fust and Schoeffer's workmen. Pannartz belonged to the

letter under Gothic influence, or a gothic letter under Roman influence, it is hard to say. In general effect it was certainly greatly inferior to the Sweynheym and Pannartz types. In all three fonts, whatever the form of lower-case letter, the capitals were distinctly roman. Many roman types of varying degrees of purity and attractiveness were used by Italian printers of this period. It was reserved for John and Wendelin de Spire to show a roman type which

12

diocese of Cologne. The theory that both men were refugees from Mainz in 1462, that Nicolas Jenson accompanied them in their flight, and that he cut the font used by them at Subiaco, as well as that subsequently employed at Rome, has been advanced by reputable authorities. Be that as it may, a very beautiful type was

produced at Subiaco, which appears to us gothic, but which they probably considered roman; for these printers, accustomed to gothic types, found themselves in a country where manuscripts in the Humanistic character were the fashion. So, while their type has many details of Gothic design in it, it has roman capitals, and lower-case letters very roman in structure, though their thickness of line gives, in the mass, the effect of gothic type. There is, too,

Jenson also used a gothic letter. He printed about a hundred and fifty books in some ten years, and as he prospered in the enterprise we may draw from his history the unexpected moral that if only a man does a thing well enough, it will reward him, in reputation, or in money, and perhaps in both. For Jenson in his own day had a great reputation, both as a publisher and printer. He died at Rome, in 1480, whither he went at the invitation of Pope Sixtus IV. Jenson's material passed into the hands of Torresano of Venice, father-in-law of Aldus, who, after the latter's death, carried on the Aldine printing-house. At the head of a broadside advertisement of various classes of books, printed (in bold gothic type) by Jenson and his associate and successor, Herbort, and brought out by the latter not many months, it is believed, after Jenson's death, there are some prefatory remarks which were perhaps written by a theologian of a Humanistic turn of mind. We quote them as a testimony to the esteem that Jenson's work enjoyed *in its own day: even allowing for the exaggeration incident to advertising. After an invocation to Christ the Illuminator of the World, it reads: "It has appeared to me to be an undertaking which would redound to the common advantage of all men, that I should in this little discourse of mine set forth to every people the extreme usefulness of the works printed in the famous city of Venice, especially of those which are from the excellent workshop of Master Nicolas Jenson the Frenchman. And in order that what*

to-day appears roman to us. In the font used in the Venice editions of Cicero's 'Epistulae ad Familiares' and Pliny's 'Historia Naturalis' of John de Spire, printed in 1469, and the 'De Civitate Dei' printed in the next year by John and Wendelin de Spire this very modern quality can be quite clearly recognized. Nicolas Jenson, whose celebrated roman types

are now to be considered, was a Frenchman, a native of Sommevoire, Haute-Marne, and for some time was mint-master-at Tours. The legend is, that Charles VII of France sent Jenson, in 1458, to Mainz, to inform himself on the subject of the new art of printing and to acquire sufficient knowledge to work in it on his return. But if Jenson ever went to Mainz, he never returned to France, and we find him in 1468 at Venice. The first roman characters, which were used by John de Spire, and

a certain amount of white between the lines of type, which results in a clearness usually characteristic of books printed in roman fonts. While not a roman type as we should now understand the term, it is, in spite of its general effect, a font well on the way thereto. Three books were printed at Subiaco–Cicero's 'De Oratore' (which, though undated, is generally considered the first one), appearing either at the end of 1464 or the beginning of 1465; the 'Opera' of Lactantius, printed in 1465; and the 'De Civitate Dei' of St. Augustine, finished in 1467. Possibly earlier than all of these was a Donatus, of which no copy exists, but of which there is a record. The end of the year 1467 finds Sweynheym and Pannartz in Rome, where they set up a press in the Palace of the De' Massimi family. Their first book printed in Rome was Cicero's 'Epistulae ad Familiares' of 1467, followed by the Lactantius of 1468. These were set in a new font which, though far less attractive than the Subiaco letter, was a much more roman type. Besides the books at Subiaco (four, if we count the Donatus) they printed about fifty at Rome, where they worked together until 1473. A roman type was also produced at Rome in 1468 by Ulrich Han for editions of Cicero's 'De Oratore' and 'Tusculanae Quaestiones,' but whether it was a roman

for which De Spire obtained an exclusive privilege for five years, have been sometimes attributed to Jenson. In any case, De Spire's death in 1470 lifted the restrictions on roman types from other Venetian printing-houses, and Jenson produced in that year his famous roman letter. The tractate 'De Praeparatione Evangelica' of Eusebius is generally considered his first book. If we look at the best Humanistic manuscripts of the period, it is readily seen whence he derived his inspiration. The characteristics of Jenson's font were its readability, its mellowness of form, and the evenness of colour in mass. Analyzed closely, his letter-forms were not very perfect; had they been so, their effect would not have been so good; for, as an authority has said, "a type too ideal in its perfection is not an ideal type." The eye becomes tired when each character is absolutely perfect. Thus the good effect of the type in mass depends somewhat upon the variations in, and consequent "movement" of, its integral parts. Jenson's roman types have been the accepted models for roman letters ever since he made them, and, repeatedly copied in our own day, have never been equalled. There were other printers in Italy whose types rivalled his, but no other man produced quite so fine a font, or had better taste in the composition of a page and its imposition upon paper. The presswork of his volumes is perhaps their weakest point. Apparently a lighter ink was used for his roman than for his gothic types—for

```
A B C D E F G H I J K L M N O
B                               P
C   A B C D E F G H I J K       Q
D   B   a b c d e f g h i   L   R
E   C   b       a b c d e   j   S
F   D   c       f g h i j   k   T
G   E   d       l m n o p   l   U
H   F   e       q r s t u   m   V
I   G   f       v w x y z   n   W
J   H   g                   o   X
K   I   h i j k l m n o p   p   Y
L   J   K U V W X Y Z A B   S   Z
M   K                       T
N O P R S T U V W X Y Z A
```

(9) A much more satisfactory arrangement of smaller sizes in this page from "On Type Faces" showing the Cloister type done two years after the Garamond opposite.

Narcissus Roman

ABCDEFGHIJK
LMNOPQRSTU
VWXYZ
ÆŒ

abcdefghijklmn
opqrstuvwxyzæ
œ ff ff fi fl ft : , ! ? " " &
(1 2 3 4 5 6 7 8 9 0)

VENETIAN

ABCDEFGHIJKLMNOP *36*
abcdefghijklmnopqrstuvwx
QRSTUVWXYZ ABCDEFGHIJ *30*
yz abcdefghijklmnopqrstuvwxyz &
ABCDEFGHIJKLMNOPQRST ABCDE *24*
abcdefghijklmnopqrstuvwxyz abcdefghijkl
ABCDEFGHIJKLMNOPQRSTUVWXYZ ABCDEF *18*
abcdefghijklmnopqrstuvwxyz 1234567890
.,:;!?''-()[]—fifflffi—ÆŒæœ

On the greatest and most useful of all inventions—the invention of alphabetical writing—Plato did not look with much complacency. He seems to have thought that the use of letters had operated on the human mind as the use of the go-cart in learning to walk, or of corks in learning to swim is said to operate on the human body. It was a support which soon became indispensable to those who used it—which made vigorous exertion first unnecessary and then impossible. The powers of the intellect would, he conceived, have been more fully developed without this delusive aid. Men would have been compelled to exercise the understanding and the memory, and, by deep and assiduous meditation, to make truth thoroughly their own. Now, on the contrary, much knowledge is traced on paper, but little is engraved in the soul. A man is certain

PLANTIN

ABCDEFGHIJKLMNOP *36*
abcdefghijklmnopqrstuvwx
QRSTUVWXYZABCDEFGHIJ *30*
yzabcdefghijklmnopqrstuvwyxzab
KLMNOPQRSTUVWXYZ ABCDEFG *24*
cdefghijklmnopqrstuvwxyzabcdefghijklmn
HIJKLMNOPQRSTUVWXYZ ABCDEFGHIJKLM *18*
abcdefghijklmnopqrstuvwxyz 1234567890
.,:;!?''-()[]—fifflffiffl&ÆŒæœ

On the greatest and most useful of all inventions—the invention of alphabetical writing—Plato did not look with much complacency. He seems to have thought that the use of letters had operated on the human mind as the use of the go-cart in learning to walk, or of corks in learning to swim is said to operate on the human body. It was a

On the greatest and most useful of all inventions—the invention of alphabetical writing—Plato did not look with much complacency. He seems to have thought that the use of letters had operated on the human mind as the use of the go-cart in learning to walk, or of corks in learning to swim is said to operate on the human body. It was a support which

33

(10, 11, 12, 13 and 14). These five pages from "On Type Faces" provide ample evidence of Morison's developing inventiveness in page layout. Walter Tiemann's Narcissus and Goudy's Forum are good examples of how an open layout allows the full character to be appreciated.

---

48 FORUM TYPE
CAPITALS ONLY
A B C D E F G H
I J K L M N O P
Q R S T U V
W X Y Z

I
2 3
4 5 & 6 7
8 9
0

36 FORUM 10 TO 48 POINT
A B C D E F G H I J K L

96

KENNERLEY ROMAN AND ITALIC

18 THAT wherein God himself is happy, the holy Angels are happy, in whose defect the Devils are unhappy—that dare I call Happiness: whatsoever conduceth unto this, may with an easy metaphor, deserve that name; whatsoever else the world terms Happiness, is to me a story out of Pliny, an apparition or neat delusion, wherein there is no more of happiness than the name. Certainly there is no happiness within this circle of flesh, nor is it in the optics of these eyes to behold felicity.

14 *INJUSTICE in this world is not something comparative; the wrong is deep, clear, and absolute in each private fate. A bruised child wailing in the street, his small world for the moment utterly black and cruel before him, does not fetch his unhappiness from sophisticated comparisons or irrational envy; nor can any compensations and celestial harmonies supervening later ever expunge or justify that moment's bitterness. ... Ignoring that pain will not prevent its having existed; it must remain for ever to trouble God's omniscience and be a part of that hell which the creation too truly involves.*

12 THAT soul that is accustomed to direct herself to God upon every occasion; that, as a flower at sun-rising, conceives a sense of God in every beam of his, and spreads and dilates itself towards him in a thankfulness, in every small blessing that he sheds upon her; that soul, that as a flower at the sun's declining, contracts and gathers in, and shuts up herself as though she had received a blow, whensoever she hears her Saviour wounded by an oath or blasphemy or execration; that soul, who, whatsoever string be strucken in her, base or treble, her high or her low estate, is ever tuned toward God—that soul prays sometimes when it does not know that it prays.

12 *I am afraid she will soon grow common to my imagination, as well as worthless in herself. Her image seems fast 'going into the wastes of time,' like a weed that the wave bears farther and farther from me. Alas! thou poor hapless weed, when I entirely lose sight of thee, and forever, no flower will ever bloom on earth to glad my heart again!*

10 AS the world is the whole frame of the world, God hath put into it a reproof, a rebuke lest it should seem eternal, which is a sensible decay and age in the whole frame of the world and every piece thereof. The seasons of the year irregular and distempered; the sun fainter and languishing; men less in stature and shorter lived. No addition, but only every year new sorts, new species of worms and flies and sicknesses, which argue more and more putrefaction of which they are engendered.

TO find a languishing wretch in a sordid corner, not only in a penurious fortune, but in an oppressed conscience, his eyes under a diverse infatuation, smothered with smoke, and smothered with tears; his ears estranged from all salutations, and visits, and all sounds but his own sighs, and the storms and thunders and earthquakes of his own despair; to enable this man to open his eyes and see that Christ Jesus stands before him ... to how down those heavens, and bring them into his sad chamber,

74

8 point

The roman letter is divided by typographers into three main divisions: the venetian, the old face, and the modern. The venetian is the somewhat square letter distinguished by heavy serifs employed by Jensen and Aldus in fifteenth-century Venice. The old face is the creation of Claude Garamond, the cele-

8 point leaded

brated French typefounder, who cut letters for the Estiennes and for Christopher Plantin. The merit of his types was immediately recognized, and many imitations (Dutch, French, and even English) sprang up. The old face defeated the venetian

9 point

In 1720 Caslon turned seriously to typefounding. He cut during the following six years several sizes of the magnificent roman and italic letter which now bear his name. It was time, indeed, that a native genius should attempt the much needed improvement

12 point

He looked anxiously for a boat to ferry him across to the other bank, when a beautiful barge approached and greeted his expectant eyes. Decks of silver and lamps of gold, sails of silk and cabins decked with canopies of satin! It was a fairy barge manned by a crew all clothed in white. Ranjhu approached the boatmen reverently, and humbly making his obeisance, persuaded them to let him rest in the boat for a while. But he was soon dragged out of bed; for, hearing of the boatmen's impertinence, Hir had arrived and ordered the immediate expulsion of the bold stranger. Presently his anger vanished, for, at the very sight of Ranjhu, Hir fell madly in love with him and became oblivious of all else. She called Ranjhu to herself, fully apologized for her rudeness, offered her hospitality to him, and finally avowed her love for him. He, in his turn, confessed how he was smitten by her beauty. Yet another case of love at first sight, and subsequent clandestine meetings, which, however, were soon discovered. The result was expulsion for Ranjhu and a forced marriage for Hir with one Khero, of Rangpur. Like Suhni, Hir would have nothing to do with her husband. She gave up food and drink, and was always in mourning. Ranjhu, on the other hand, wandered about in the garb of an ascetic, longing for a sight of Hir. Good luck brought him to Rangpur, where he managed to meet Hir, and flee with her, through the good offices of her sister-in-law, Sahti. They were, however, pursued, brought back and tried, before the local Kazi (magistrate), whose verdict was immediate exile for Ranjhu and the compulsory return of Hir to her husband's house, near Jhang Siyal.

8 point

in the appearance English printing, si the market had for ve long been dependent up foreign-made types, which only the m inferior were sent to o printers. The success William Caslon's let was instant, and been continuous ev since, if we except period of sixty ye from 1780 to 1840.

8 point leaded

The scholar only kn how dear these sile yet eloquent, compani (books) of pure thoug and innocent hours come in the seasons adversity. When that is worldly turns dross around us, th only retain their stea value. When frien

9 point

grow cold and t converse of intima languishes into vaf civility and commo place, these only co tinue the unalter countenance of happ days, and cheer with that true frien ship which nev deceived hope n deserted sorrow.

Washington Irvi

11 point

THE SHEPHERD TO THE FLOWERS

SWEET VIOLETS, Love's paradise, that spread
Your gracious odours, which you couched bear
Within your paly faces,
Upon the gentle wing of some calm-breathing wind
That plays amidst the plain,
If by the favour of propitious stars you gain
Such grace as in my lady's bosom-place to find;
Be proud to touch those places.   [wear,
And when her warmth your moisture forth doth
Whereby her dainty parts are sweetly fed;
You honours of the flowery meads I pray,
You pretty daughters of the earth and sun;
With mild and seemly breathing straight display
My bitter sighs that have my heart undone.
Vermilion roses, that with new day's rise

Display your crimson folds fresh-looking fair,
Whose radiant bright disgraces
The rich adorned rays of roseate rising morn;
Ah! if her virgin's hand
Do pluck your pure ere Phœbus view the land,
And vail your gracious pomp in lovely Nature's sc
If chance my mistress traces
Fast by your flowers to take the summer's air;
Then woeful blushing tempt her glorious eyes,
To spread their tears, Adonis' death reporting,
And tell love's torments, sorrowing for her friends
Whose drops of blood within your leaves consorting
Report fair Venus' moans to have no end.
Then may remorse in pitying of my smart,
Dry up my tears, and dwell within her heart.

(15) Smaller sizes of Caslon Old Face from "On Type Faces". In the left hand column and top right, more of Morison's historical notes.

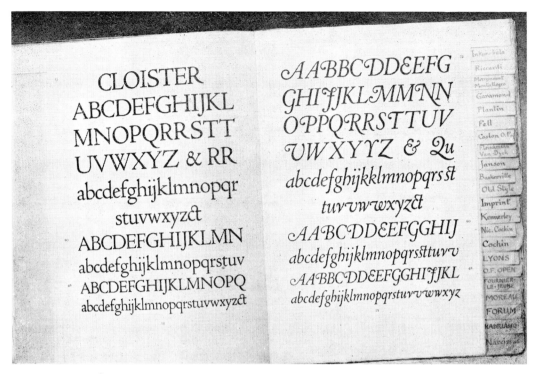

(16) This double page spread from "On Type Faces", a royal quarto volume, shows an ideal treatment for larger sizes. The handmade thumb index on the fore-edge was done by Frank Sidgwick and gave a hint to designers of type specimen books.

In addition this page also has a slip pasted on it which reads: "Page 11, line 11, delete (Whose Venezia is shown elsewhere in this volume)." This phrase occurs in the introduction to the Cloister specimen and we must conclude that it was originally intended to include the George W. Jones's Venezia face in the book, which would have meant that besides handset foundry types being shown, both mechanical typesetting systems would have been represented in the list of "type for printing of books" and thus bringing a prestige to the Linotype system Jones had shown it to merit.

But, as it happened, Venezia did not become available in a full range on the Linotype until some years later. Venezia was also made available for hand-setting by Stephenson Blake.

Morison also designed some specimen sheets for the Fanfare Press (about which there is more later). The size of these sheets was $13\frac{1}{4}$ inches by $9\frac{1}{4}$ inches, quite an arbitrary choice having no relation to a standard paper size, and the sheets were intended for a loose-leaf binder, each type being set out on a single sheet or allowed to run to as many pages as necessary. Morison did

several of these, and he took the work very seriously in spite of being heavily
committed elsewhere. He designed the Caslon sheet and wrote the introductory note, boldly describing it as the English Old Face, and chose the passages
for the setting of the actual specimen. Few people can have escaped the frustra-
tion that comes from reading the texts chosen for specimen settings only to be
stopped in the middle of some fascinating description or piece of information
with no indication of its source. Morison's settings are no exception and to
trace them all would require the services of a librarian.

It was therefore a lot of hard experience that assured Morison a confident
mood in which to design specimens for the Monotype Corporation when he
became connected with that admirable organisation then so important in the
printing industry.

"The Monotype Corporation issued some fine publicity explaining their
new type faces" states a laconic note in the British Museum's catalogue of the
exhibition it put on as a tribute to Morison. "Explaining" is an unusual word
in relation to type faces and it recalls Pavlova's remark when asked to
"explain" her dancing. "If I could explain it" she is supposed to have replied,
"I would not need to dance."

The BM sentence is a splendid example of the national talent for under-
statement for "fine publicity" was, to use a current catchphrase, the name of
the game, a game at which the Monotype Corporation in the person of Mrs.
Beatrice Warde, its publicity manager, played to perfection, supported con-
stantly by Morison's friendship and knowledge. But that is another story.

To show all the typography that Morison did or influenced at Monotype
would need an encyclopedia. Two booklets and another broadsheet will do to
reveal the skill and taste he had developed in a few years of concentration on
the perfection of detail which is the secret of fine typography. The designing
of a book of type specimens is by no means the same thing as designing an
extensive specimen of a single type face. The same basic layout can be adequately repeated for a collection of types since it is intended more as a record
of what is available. The specimen of a single type should completely reveal
its character to help the typographer to form an opinion of it. Every practising
typographer knows that it takes time to achieve perfect control of any type
face. For my part I can truthfully say that it is only Caslon over which I feel
I have complete mastery. In typography it is not just a matter of making a
good layout and then deciding what type should be used. One has to know
every letter and the different effects of capitals and lower case, a sureness of
the colour of different sizes in the mass.

In the case of Garamond it is safe to say that Morison had mastered this
particular design beyond all doubt. We have already seen earlier in this

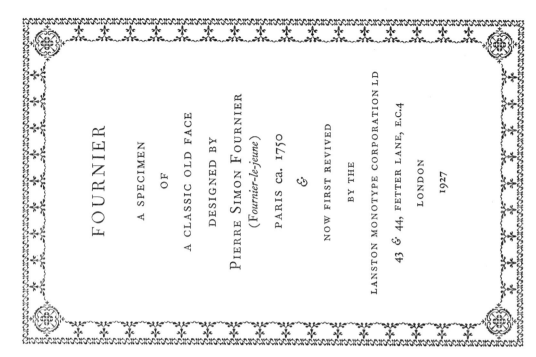

FOURNIER

A SPECIMEN

OF

A CLASSIC OLD FACE

DESIGNED BY

PIERRE SIMON FOURNIER

(*Fournier-le-jeune*)

PARIS ca. 1750

&

NOW FIRST REVIVED

BY THE

LANSTON MONOTYPE CORPORATION LD

43 & 44, FETTER LANE, E.C.4

LONDON

1927

THE GARAMOND TYPE

Roman and Italic

A FIRST SHOWING

From the CLOISTER PRESS, *Heaton Mersey*

(17) Anxious to be the first English printer to announce its acquisition of the ATF Garamond in 1921 the Cloister Press put out a small leaflet showing five smaller sizes. The clue to Morison's hand, the two paragraph marks laid sideways. (18) The title page of the Monotype specimen book of Fournier six years later has a greater sophistication in its arrangement of text and ornament.

GARAMOND

A SPECIMEN
of a classic face reproduced for use on the
" MONOTYPE "
Six sizes, 12 to 36 point

LONDON : PRINTED BY
THE LANSTON MONOTYPE CORPORATION, LTD
43 & 44, FETTER LANE, E.C.4
1923

(19 and 20) By the time he went to Monotype Morison had acquired a confidence in his typography as the specimens from then on exhibit, and which he never lost; it is seen at its best in the title pages of the booklets for Garamond and Baskerville.

A SPECIMEN

OF

PRINTING LETTER

DESIGNED BY

John Baskerville

ABOUT THE YEAR MDCCLVII

RECUT BY

THE LANSTON

MONOTYPE CORPORATION

LIMITED FOR USE ON THE

"MONOTYPE"

LONDON

43 AND 44 FETTER LANE E.C.4

MCMXXVI

NOTICE
to
THE READER

*

The square Italian variety of type, with its slab serifs, was succeeded by that known to us as "old face." The former letter was wrought to perfection by craftsmen of Venice, a city which long enjoyed the primacy of typographical honour. The perfected types of the brothers da Spira, and of Nicolas Jenson (1492), were widely copied, as was the italic later brought out by Aldus (1501). The more, as in respect to type, lay-out, format, paper

A NOTE

ON THE BASKERVILLE TYPE

THIS *new "Monotype" face is a faithful reproduction of an historic type designed by John Baskerville, the Birmingham ex-footman and writing master, who was born in 1706. His interest in typography dates from 1750, and during twenty-five years he printed and published a large number of editions of English, Latin and Greek classics in octavo and quarto, and one or two folios which by reason of the fineness of paper (he was one of the first if not the first, to use wove) and type employed exerted a tremendous influence upon English and foreign typography.*

(21) Silent instruction in the appropriate use of ornament in the Garamond and Baskerville specimen booklets. Above left, flowers of the period for the classic Garamond; right, more formal, geometric ornament for the transitional Baskerville. (22) The correctness of this choice is plain when the ornament is transposed (below).

NOTICE
to
THE READER

*

The square Italian variety of type, with its slab serifs, was succeeded by that known to us as "old face." The former letter was wrought to perfection by craftsmen of Venice, a city which long enjoyed the primacy of typographical honour. The perfected types of the brothers da Spira, and of Nicolas Jenson (1492), were widely copied, as was the italic later brought out by Aldus (1501). The more, as in respect to type, lay-out, format, paper and binding, the Venetian editions excelled all

A NOTE

ON THE BASKERVILLE TYPE

THIS *new "Monotype" face is a faithful reproduction of an historic type designed by John Baskerville, the Birmingham ex-footman and writing master, who was born in 1706. His interest in typography dates from 1750, and during twenty-five years he printed and published a large number of editions of English, Latin and Greek classics in octavo and quarto, and one or two folios which by reason of the fineness of paper (he was one of the first if not the first, to use wove) and type employed exerted a tremendous influence upon English and foreign typography.*

A B C D E F

B   G

C   H

THE
ENGLISH
OLD·FACE

is identified with the name of
William Caslon who cut the series between the years 1720 and
1726. In design the type is
simple and unaffected, express-
ing dignity and charm. It is an
eighteenth century letter, and
therefore somewhat conservative
in feeling; but it may be re-
lied upon to impart an agreeable
straightforwardness to any composition in which it is used. Mr.
C.W.Hobson's composing room
contains eleven sizes of this letter of which the following pages
form a specimen

1926

D   I

E   J

F   K

G   L

H   M

I   N

J K L M N O

(23) In designing the Caslon Old Face specimen for The Fanfare press Morison courageously excluded the familiar flowers or any attempt to convey a period style. The result was a fresh look at this timeless design. (Original 13¼ ins. by 9¼ ins.)

THE

LANSTON   MONOTYPE

CORPORATION, LTD.

have the pleasure to announce that

THE GARAMOND TYPE

is now ready in six sizes, 12 to 36 point
as follows :

ABCDEF abcdefghijklmnopqr

ABCDEFGabcdefghijklmnopqrst

HIJKLMNabcdefghijklmnopqrstuvw

HIJKLMN abcdefghijklmnopqrstuvwxyz

OPQRSTUV abcdefghijklmnopqrstuvwxyz

NOPQRSTUV& abcdefghijklmnopqrstuvwxyz

WXYZABabcdefghijklmnopqrstuvwxyz& 1234567890 £

ABCDEFGHIJKL abcdefghijklmnopqrstuvwxyz 1234567890ſt

ABCDEFGHIJKLMNOabcdefghijklmnopqrstuvwxyz1234567890£ & ſtⅇt

ABCDEFGHIJKLMNOPQRSTUVWXYZ abcdefghijklmnopqrstuvwxyzisⅇt

ABCDEFGHIJKLMNOPQRSTUVabcdefghijklmnopqrstuvwxyz ſtⅇt 1234567890£

ABCDEFGHIJKLMNOPQRST UVWXYZ abcdefghijklmnopqrstuvwxyz ſpſtas Qu&

et nt ℮ m, as is us ij ⅇt ſt ſp fr gy k tt ll ta v q, ſa ſe ſi ſo ſu ſæ ſc ſs ſt ſſ ſſa ſſe ſſi ſſo ſſu

Ex Na Ne Ni No Nu Ra Re Ri Ro Ru

A B C D E G H J M

P T V QU Qu Qu

THE LANSTON MONOTYPE CORPORATION, LTD
43 & 44, FETTER LANE, LONDON, E.C.4

A SPECIMEN OF "MONOTYPE" BELL

SERIES NUMBER 341

The founts displayed in ten sizes on this specimen sheet are reproductions of a Set of New Types originally engraved between the years 1787 and 1789 under the direction of the most enterprising publisher and typographer of his generation, John Bell, 1745-1831

36-POINT

He was ambitious to surpass the finest achievements of the best of the Continental printers, *François Ambroise Didot*, of Paris, and *Giambattista Bodoni*, of Parma, as well as the work of his forerunner at home, John Baskerville, of Birmingham, whose folio Bible was published at Cambridge at the time that *John Bell*, as a young man, was about to open the *The British Library* in the Strand, London

30-POINT

JOHN BELL attracted notice first as one of the proprietors and conductors of the *Morning Post* newspaper, founded November 2, 1772, and still in progress at the present day. Later he joined with Captain Edward Topham in a new daily entitled *The World*. In 1788 he published his twenty-volume *Shakspere*, with copper-engraved illustrations

24-POINT

Bell's Edition of Shakspere, issued under the patronage of His Royal Highness George Prince of Wales, was able to grace its subscription list with the names of half the Royal family of England and of Her Most Christian Majesty the Queen of France

18-POINT

COMPOSITION MATRICES

The preface to *Bell's Edition of Shakspere* indicated that in point of exterior "it is believed that it hath as yet no rival, either in ornaments, printing or paper". There was one important novelty which affected all subsequent printing. In the words of the preface, the editor "in the mode of printing too, hath ventured to depart from one common mode, by rejecting the long s in favour of the round one, as being less liable to error from the occasional imperfections of the letter f, and the frequent substitution of it for the long s; the regularity of the print is by that means very much promoted, the lines having the effect of being more open, without being at any additional distance"

14-POINT

In 1788 John Bell issued his first specimen of type from the British Letter Foundry. These types were cut by Richard Austin. Attention was called to these beautiful types, still in the possession of Messrs. Stephenson, Blake and Co., Ltd., by Mr. Stanley Morison in an article in *The Fleuron* No. 5. Here Mr. Morison calls it "our first independent design" and says that "while maintaining its predominantly old-face character exhibits tendencies towards the modern face". It is significant that Bell was in Paris in 1785 visiting the printers and typefounders. The type may have been inspired there.

8-POINT

John Bell issued the original prospectus of his own type from his new printing letter foundry in May, 1788. He wrote that he intended to produce "an original cast of Types from punches cut upon new, and I flatter myself, very improved principles!" He proposed to issue a Book of Common Prayer in such a style as to render it in every respect the most perfect and most beautiful book that ever was produced in any country. "*On this work I hope to hold my fame as a letter founder and printer.*" Paper, presswork and type were to be ideally related.

12-POINT

ABCDEFGHIJKLMNOPQQRRSTUVW
12345 XYZ& 67890
ABCDEFGHIJKKLMNOPQRRSTUVWXYZ
ABCDEFGHIJKKLMNOPQRRSTUVW
XYZ& AJNQY
abcdefghijkklmnopqrstuvwxyz
The serifs are flat, but bracketed and delicately shaped. The designer has supplied the roman with two K's, two Q's, and two R's, one curly tailed; and the italic with alternative *AJNQY* and *T*. In the lower-case there are kk, *kk*, and *bb*. 9-POINT

The lower-case e, with the remarkably low cross stroke and with the conspicuous counter, is paralleled in the handsome founts engraved by François Ambroise Didot. The capital R, with the curly tail, which Baskerville occasionally used, and Caslon never, originated with Granjean. Fournier had it, and of course Didot. Bell invented an alternative K with a curly tail. In the lower-case an alternative k with a curly tail is given in both roman and italic. The short-ranging J which had been introduced by Granjean in the *romain du roi* of 1693 and cut by Fournier-le-jeune in 1763, appears here for the first time in England—though Bell gives also the descending J. The figures are another novelty; the old style "hanging" sorts are deserted in favour of what are known to printers as modern or ranging figures.

9-POINT

The fount was engraved according to the directions of John Bell by a young copperplate artist-craftsman who worked for instrument-makers, seal-cutters, tool-makers, die-stampers and the like. His name was *Richard Austin*. The Bell fount has the aspect and the pretensions of one of F. A. Didot's types but it is sharper in feature and more abruptly contrasted as between its thicks and thins. The serifs are calculated for producing a fine effect upon the new and delicate silky wove paper which Bell was determined to use. *That the Bell fount is the first English Modern Face is proved by inspection of sizes above fourteen point.* The serif structure readily distinguishes from Old Face.

11-POINT

The quality of the engraving is remarkable, surpassing all previous English and continental type-cutting in precision. Bodoni had familiarised England and Europe with a flat serif taken from Granjean's *romain du roi*, and with sharply contrasted thicks and thins. It is, therefore, much to the credit of Bell and Austin that they have maintained their independence equally against Bodoni and Baskerville. For all its French influence, the Bell type looks English and is English because it is conservative, yet not more conservative than it behoved an eighteenth-century typefounder to be. The type possesses a harmony in serif formation as between roman and italic not possessed by the average French type.

10-POINT

LONDON: THE MONOTYPE CORPORATION LTD., 43 FETTER LANE, E.C.4

Registered MONOTYPE *Trade Mark*

A COPY OF THIS SPECIMEN, PRINTED AS AN UNCREASED BROADSIDE ON RAG PAPER WILL BE SENT TO ANY APPLICANT ON RECEIPT OF POST CARD

---

(24) Opposite. This display of the Monotype Garamond type (14 ins. by 9 ins.) was folded into the 1923 specimen booklet and contains a suggestion of the celebrated broadsheets that came later. (25) Above. The scholarly text and the skilful display of the Monotype broadsheets compelled perusal. Morison called Bell "the most enterprising typographer of his generation". (Original 22¼ ins. by 17¼ ins.)

chapter the two previous examples of his struggle with it—in the Cloister Press specimen sheet, and in his book *On Type Faces*.

Whereas Garamond, a sixteenth-century French type, can be described as beautiful, Baskerville, an eighteenth-century English type, is a plain type. To design specimens that bring out the fundamental differences of these two important founts is a challenge serious enough to test the most intelligent designer. It was a challenge that Morison answered with two booklets that do more to "explain" the nature of type design than any amount of writing could do.

In the case of Garamond it will be noticed that nowhere has it been leaded and indeed few typographers would consider leading this type. On the other hand all sizes of the Baskerville from eight to twenty-four point are shown leaded, and few will quarrel with the suggestion thus made in the specimen that this type could be set solid or leaded with success, providing of course both size and measure are considered.

Two further points need to be made about the Garamond and the Baskerville. The first concerns the ornament used on the inside pages. On the Garamond specimen the flowers from contemporary sources seem in complete harmony with the type but when they are put on the Baskerville page the effect is immediately unpleasing. The second point that cannot be demonstrated here concerns the choice of paper: that of the Garamond is a soft antique wove and that of the Baskerville is Basingwerk, a smooth, fairly hard surface akin to the "ironed" paper that Baskerville preferred for his own printing. These factors complete the task of demonstrating the type face which is the function of the specimen for a single face.

Of the other specimens which Morison originated for Monotype none have had a greater acclamation than the broadsheets, which are admired for their bold design and lively text, often Morison's. These items hanging in printing offices were an inspiration to many craftsmen proud of their trade and having the ambition to advance in it. One of them celebrates the type of John Bell which Morison claims as the first English Modern Face and it is due to his energetic researches that it is now a part of our typographic treasury.

3

EPHEMERA WITH A LONG LIFE

All that heterogenous printed matter politely referred to as ephemera is known in the trade as jobbing. "Jobbing work" wrote John Southward in 1899 "is a term applied to every kind of printing except bookwork and newspaper work." In this definition the earliest example of typographic printing, the 1454 Indulgence of Mainz, was a piece of jobbing printing. "Anything from a visiting card to a poster" was the slogan the jobbing printer used to advertise his business. Thus wrote Alfred Harper of Cheltenham in the authentic voice of the jobbing printer about the middle of the nineteenth century:

> Auctioneers' Bills and Catalogues, produced at the time required, however brief the notice given for its execution, at a considerable reduction on the usual charges. Address Cards, Circulars, Billheads, Labels, &c., neatly printed. Posting Bills of any dimensions printed in the most gorgeous Colours at very reasonable rate, and in a style not to be surpassed.

The key word here is style for it was the style of jobbing, which we would now call commercial printing, that, next to the concern for the standards of bookwork became the focus of interest. For style is, of course, another word for design.

Throughout the nineteenth century jobbing printing was left to compositors to construct, with the result that every job was, as nearly as the wording permitted, an imitation of a previous one. Quite often, for the main lines of a poster or a programme such as "Concert," "Dance" or "Meeting" or "catch" lines such as "on", "at" or "in," the same type was used again and again. There is a story of a compositor when faced with a job for which there was no pattern confessed: "I'm not much good at manuscript but I'm a bugger for reprint."

The displayed book title page with one line in roman capitals, one line in upper and lower case italic, one line in black letter and another line in fat face has a certain antique charm today, but it was more of necessity than a product of imagination—there were not enough letters of the larger sizes of type to allow the complete title to be set in one size. Yet the typographically variegated title page became the model for much jobbing work; the idea had been firmly planted and it took a long time to uproot.

45

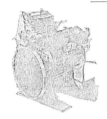

The **New Heavy Duty**
Miller Automatic Unit

The Iron Man For Service

THIS new member of the Miller family is designed for high-class work, and adds to platen press-room efficiency. With four form rollers, two vibrating rollers, and vibrating Brayer fountain, perfect ink distribution is assured. Adjustable roller tracks and foot-brake complete the efficiency of the machine

This Heavy Duty Unit is capable of doing 95% of your platen work, and shows a handsome profit on everything it does.

THE MILLER AUTOMATIC FEEDER
Feeds any Stock from Manifold to 8-sheet Boards.
There are Over 16,000 in use throughout the world.

The Lanston Monotype Corporation, Limited
[Printers' Machinery Department]   43 and 44, FETTER LANE, LONDON, E.C. 4

(26) The printer's resources, and the compositor's, in 1901; the advertiser had no literary resources and could not compose a sentence to describe his business. (27) Twenty years later copywriting has emerged and there has been some conscious attempt at layout.

Not that there weren't conscious efforts to formulate principles of type display—there were, but unfortunately they were no improvement. The centred style, the grouped style, the art style were names given to suggested methods of design all overloaded with rules and the debased Victorian ornament. The advertisement from *Jackson's Cyclists' Guide to Yorkshire* published, in 1900 belongs to no school save that of the lonely compositor who, working perhaps from copy scribbled on the back of an envelope, was sincerely trying to do his best for Messrs. Legg & Millard. For those who enjoy typographical identification and are wondering about the symbol before the letters "EEDS" in the bottom line, it is the second colour for the ornamented capital "L" in the name LEGG in the top line. This tradition of jobbing work was not confined to the supposedly less sophisticated provinces or back street printers. Its universality, and its durability, is well marked in the advertisement for the Miller equipment, handled by Monotype, which appeared in *The Monotype Recorder* for November-December 1921—twenty years after Messrs. Legg & Millard. Though it is far from perfect, the Morison inspired layout for

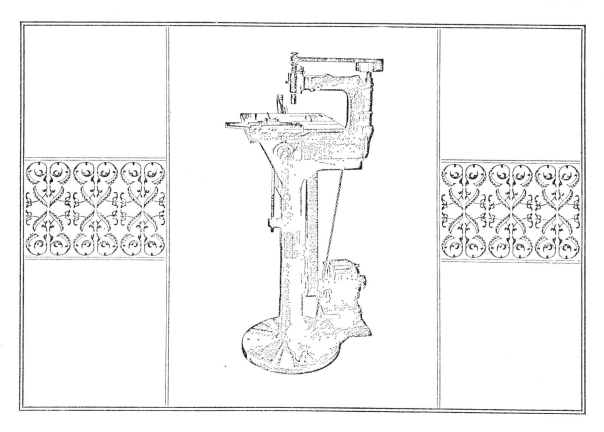

(28) Morison's rationalising influence on the 1923 layout of what is virtually the same material as in the previous illustration. The ornaments were still in vogue.

UNDER THE PATRONAGE OF
H.M. QUEEN ALEXANDRA

GUDRUN JASTRAU

AT THE DORIEN
LEIGH GALLERIES

No. 8 Bruton St., Bond St., W.

Price One Shilling

(29) Left, catalogue cover in black on pale blue paper; right, a page of text. Simple and elegant it could hardly be improved. Perhaps a modern designer would have moved the titles close to their numbers, but the open, casual feeling of the page would be lost.

Miller equipment, which appeared in *The Monotype Recorder* for September-October 1923, demonstrates the simple principle of reducing the number of elements to three: the headline (divided, for sake of emphasis); the illustration; and the text matter. Take away the ornaments each side of the illustration and the initial letter and you have a classic arrangement that could be used today.

Above all, the fancy types produced in endless profusion for display work nullified any sound advice which may have been contained in the many books and articles in the trade press on the subject. The improvement in the design of commercial printing owes something to the influence of the followers of William Morris, one of whose practical achievements was to alert public attention to the design of printing in general. It may be noted in passing that the only items of nineteenth-century jobbing printing which survive are the theatrical bills which have long had the interest of the collectors.

By the nature of the business it canvassed and advertised itself as capable of producing the Pelican Press was in printing trade terms a jobbing house, and the work that Morison designed there ranged in the traditional phrase "from a visiting card to a poster," as the illustrations in this chapter testify. This is the work on which Morison cut his teeth, always a painful process, in the course of developing a style and eventual mastery of the medium of typography. We have seen in the previous chapter the typographic resources Morison had at his command in his first job as a designer for the Pelican Press, and we can now see the work he produced with them during the two years or so he was there—roughly from March 1919 to May 1921.

In marked contrast to the style of jobbing printing which continued to be dominated by a muddle of type faces, Morison's work immediately achieved a new look by restricting the number of faces used together, and at a stroke established a unity and dignity completely absent in the past. Further, the relationship between the typeface and illustration was shown to be as important as it is acknowledged to be in bookwork. Good examples of these critical points can be seen in the cover of the catalogue for the exhibition of Gudrun Jastrau, where the Nicolas Cochin type printed in black ink on pale grey paper harmonises with the charming illustration above; in the cover of the booklet "Combination in the Food Trade" where the Moreau-le Jeune type is at one with the border. These borders redrawn from the sixteenth-century originals of Geoffrey Tory, "the greatest of all decorators of typography"[1] have an added interest as some of the units are the same as those shown in the Chiswick Press specimen book and deserve a word of explanation.

Charles Whittingham the younger, whose reputation does not entirely

---

[1] *Gutenberg to Plantin.* George Parker Winship.

PROGRAMME

¶ 1 (a) Toccata in A — *Paradies*

(b) Two Harpsichord Lessons, Nos. 19 & 10 — *Domenico Scarlatti*

IN the preface to his collection of Sonatas, Scarlatti says: "Reader, be you professor or amateur, do not expect a profound intention in my pieces; to my thinking there is no other rule in music worthy of a man of genius than to please that sense, to delight which is the object of music."

(c) Prelude and Fugue in B flat, Book I, No. 21 — *Bach*

ISIDORA ALGAR

¶ 2 (a) "Little Bateese" — *Henry Drummond* (French Canadian)

(b) "The Wreck of the Juliet Plante" " (French Canadian)

COMBINATION in the FOOD TRADE for INDUSTRIAL PROGRESS & NATIONAL ENDS

London 1920

(30 and 31) The Pelican Press made good use of their redrawn Tory and Lyons borders and showed good taste in the choice or types to go with them.

rest on having revived the Caslon types for a new edition of *Lady Willoughby's Diary* in 1844, greatly admired the work of the eighteenth-century printers, Geoffrey Tory of Paris, and Henry Bynneman and Henry Denham of London.

He taught his family to appreciate their beauty and to perpetuate it, and his daughters Charlotte and Elizabeth copied and designed head and tail pieces, borders and initial letters, while another lady, Mary Byfield, who came of a family of engravers, engraved them.[1]

It is perhaps in the "occasional" printing that Morison developed his light touch. In a booklet he designed and wrote for the Cloister Press, there are a few sentences that seem to have a retrospective quality applicable to the jobbing work of the Pelican:

Print may be beautiful because it serves a plain purpose plainly without fuss and without waste. It will have gone a long way to be beautiful if it is exquisitely legible. If it fails of these cardinal virtues it will not be beautiful and decoration will only make it worse. These than are the principles which the Cloister Press brings to the construction of a piece of good printing; perhaps a catalogue of admirable arrangement, or a poster which will flatter the eye as well as excite attention; perhaps an invitation card which will really invite, or the prettiest of programmes . . .

"The prettiest of programmes." The Pelican Press imprint appeared in many of them, such as that for the recital of Isidore Algar and Peggy Murray. One of the Pelican's customers was the Dorien Leigh Galleries which as well as selling paintings also imported "precious" papers from China, Korea, Java and Japan. These featherweight materials attracted Morison and he used them frequently, one design in particular being used on several jobs besides this one. The cover has a pasted-on label, his favourite style of external design both for books and pamphlets, and shows his careful spacing of capitals and the free use of section marks as a decorative border. Each of the inside pages has the same Lyons border to hold the text matter. Great pains have been taken to give the maximum tidiness to what is of necessity broken up copy. We do not now see the need to letterspace the words "Juliet Plante" to make the line square up when the last line in items (b) and (c) above it are allowed to be short. Perhaps it was an oversight to use paragraph marks between the items in one case and leaf ornaments in another.

The same sensitive concern for materials is evident in the Gudrun Jastrau catalogue already mentioned. In this case the material for the outer four pages is a lightweight grey-toned Hammermill Bond and that for the inside four

[1] *English Printers' Ornaments.* Henry R. Plomer.

THE PELICAN PRESS

A Branch of the VICTORIA HOUSE PRINTING CO. LTD.

2 CARMELITE STREET
LONDON, E.C.

*All business communications
to be addressed to the Firm*

*In replying
please quote* Ref.

(32 and 33) Morison enclosed this visiting card with the collection of his work he presented to Frank Sidgwick from which many of the illustrations in this chapter are taken. Although he used the same border for both letterheading and card he did not hesitate to use Cochin for one and Goudy's types for the other.

FELLOWSHIP SERVICES

MAUDE ROYDEN *and* PERCY DEARMER

Kensington Town Hall   London, W.

VOL. II.   JANUARY, 1921   No. 1

NOTES

A HAPPY New Year to everybody, and may the Fellowship Services, the Fellowship Guild, and all our friends, prosper. And may 1921 be less bitter and sorrowful than its predecessors. May we all help in the rebuilding of the new world.

NEGOTIATIONS of a delicate and private nature have been proceeding in various directions with a view to our obtaining a resting-place of our own for Fellowship Services and Fellowship activities. At the moment of going to press, unfortunately, the Committee has no definite news to impart. But there have been hopeful developments, and at any moment good news may come along, which will at once be announced to the congregation.

ENCLOSED in this New Year's Monthly Paper is a subscription form, which we hope will be filled up by those whose means enable them to do so. We owe everything to the generosity of our many friends, shown in so many ways; but we must not forget that the collections alone would not enable us to pay our way. We need also regular subscriptions; and it is the greatest help to the Treasurer to have some idea at the beginning of the year as to what he may expect during the next twelve months. Do not hesitate to fill in small amounts if you cannot afford more; and do not think you must put something down if you are unable to afford it. The form can be given in at the bookstall or handed to Mr. Pomeroy or one of the stewards.

THE voluntary choir, which is drawn from the congregation and sits among the congregation, is proving of the greatest use in helping the congregational singing, of which we are becoming very proud. There is a

---

(34) Printed on antique wove this four-page leaflet had the period look Morison and Meynell aimed to achieve. The capitals at the head are those cut by Gill for Burns and Oates some years earlier and their uneven alignment is due to being individually cut on wood though it adds to the effect.

pages an equally lightweight antique wove, sewn with a two-hole thread stitch. It weighs less than an ounce and the physical impression is of holding something precious. A marked disregard of the conventional was apparent in his work even in the design of his own business card and the letterheading for the Pelican Press. To the trade a business card was an extra thirds card (3 inches by $1\frac{3}{4}$ inches), with script lettering die-stamped on a 2-sheet ivory board. Morison's card did not conform to any standard size, it was set in the Kennerley type and printed by letterpress on a piece of yellow cover paper with a linen finish. The letterheading, perhaps the first to have a flower border, was medium quarto instead of the more usual large post quarto. It should be noted that the flower border on the business card is the same as that used on the letterheading; is this Morison unconsciously pioneering "matching" stationery?

The reward for taking an unprejudiced look at a proposed piece of printing is shown in the leaflet for *The National Review*. Here a simple advertising leaflet has acquired an impressive feeling by disregarding the usual formula. Some suggestion may have been made to the client about the wording which has been reduced to two grammatical sentences set out with a minimum of display in a rational, easily read form. Because the outline type has the character associated with engraving, it has a look of importance. Again, a light brown laid stock, with a hint of the crackle of handmade paper, has added a physically attractive element.

Quite often the printer has to give printed form to a job for which he has no precedent as regards style (we are back to our frank compositor), and even though the work may be of minor importance the conscientious typographer accepts the challenge. The result of this approach is that the receipt form for the Fellowship Service Fund both in its language and its typography has a pleasant look with no suggestion of an official form. Jobbing printing differs to this extent from book printing in that there is no classic period in the sense of being the ideal or perfect model. Morison got near it in creating an ephemera that resisted any attempt to throw it away. Of the Pelican Press work as a whole James Moran wrote:[1] "it was responsible for a much needed revitalising of typography in the commercial field," praise which Morison would have been happy to share with his friend and partner Francis Meynell. Fifty years later in his autobiography[2] Meynell wrote: "Looking today at the adventurous pieces of promotion we produced for the Pelican, I wonder if Morison and I did as well for our customers as we did for the typographical revival and our own enterprises."

[1] *Stanley Morison: his typographic achievement.* (Lund Humphries.)
[2] *My Lives.* (The Bodley Head.)

IT IS COMMON GROUND that the intelligence of the country is in revolt against professional politicians of all Parties, whether Labour, Radical or Coalition.

If you wish to understand why, you should read regularly

THE

NATIONAL REVIEW Edited by L. J. MAXSE. Monthly, 3s. net. Published at 43 Duke St., St. James', S.W.1

Pelican Press

(35) Most of Morison's typography at the Pelican Press was on traditional lines; here is an example of his unorthodoxy. Original printed in black on light brown Fabriano paper.

The last job Morison did for Pelican was a house job, a promotional piece for the Press, entitled *The Craft of Printing*. It claimed to be no more than an "elementary summary of the history of type-forms . . . addressed to the buyer of printing" but it was, in the mind of his biographer, Nicolas Barker, "the first draft of an enquiry which had already engaged Morison for over ten years and was to occupy him for the rest of his life."[1] In less than two thousand words it gives a credible history of type forms from Gutenberg to William Morris. In production it approaches fine printing in typography and press-work, and it is one of those of its items that the Pelican claimed had become museum pieces.

The Craft of Printing was also the title given to a supplement to the *Manchester Guardian* of May 23, 1922, described as "A Brief Review of the Progress and Present State of the Printing Arts arranged, designed and produced at the Cloister Press." All the articles are unsigned but "The History of Printing Types" is Morison's. The format, $18\frac{1}{4}$ inches by $11\frac{3}{4}$ inches, which did so much to give it its authoritative character is likely to have been proposed by him. So too was the use of the Plantin type which has given the strong colour necessary to the large page that no other face available for machine setting at the time could have done.

The easy-going atmosphere at the Pelican Press suited Morison's character perfectly. He was virtually his own master, free to design as he pleased with Francis Meynell happy to approve completely all he did. Charles W. Hobson of the Cloister Press, his next employer, was by contrast a dominant character who let no one remain for long in doubt as to who was in charge. Besides the printing plant in Heaton Mersey he had an advertising agency in Manchester which was already turning out some of the best advertising in the country. He eventually brought the agency to London and he had grandiose ideas for a vast centre of printing and associated activities, but he does not appear to have fully divulged them to anyone.

Hobson, a cultured man, had a collection of well-printed books in which he used to see typographic treatments he liked, and he would tell William Grimmond, a talented but untemperamental artist and typographer, what to do on a specific job. The point was that the resourceful Grimmond could do all that was asked of him and did so willingly. It happened that Ernest Ingham (of whom much more later) was on Hobson's staff at this time and believes that in some cases it is impossible to say for certain whether a job was designed by Morison or Grimmond. Moreover, according to Ingham, Morison seldom appeared in the office of the Hobson agency where most of the work was designed. And since in any event Morison's stay in Manchester lasted only a

[1] *Stanley Morrison*, Nicolas Barker. (Macmillan.)

(36) A bookplate for Professor Minns whom Morison met in the course of researches for his book "Politics and Script".
(37) Characteristically neat Pelican Press setting for a gallery catalogue. And that blind paragraph mark with the curled tail!

LIBER ELLIS H · MINNS LITT · D ·
AUL · PEMB · ET ACAD · BRIT · SOC ·
PALAEOGRAPHIAE OLIM LECTORIS
ARCHAEOLOGIAE PROF · DISNEIANI

THE LIVING THEATRE

A living Theatre is that in which all is alive with a life not to be found in the day's rounds.
It is the one theatre which cannot be imitated, for it is alive.
Is the living Theatre a thanksgiving of song and motion?
Do we see and hear the mountains breathing and trilling?
Do the rivers and the rains enter before us?
Or what? Neat Little Egoists acting or the Gods? I ask?

SCENE—ALIVE

1 The Temple
2 "Gibbon"
3 Child Hidden
4 Little Tomb
5 Sentinel
6 "Light"
7 Hell
8 Descending into the Tomb
9 Hades
10 Dancers
11 Masked Man
12 The Revolution
13 Neobe
14 Ueber—Marionette
15 The Young Woman
16 "Child Roland to the Dark Tower Came"

¶

BLACK FIGURES—MARIONETTES

After the scene—the figures.
> These figures belong to the scene, and you must be left to decide for yourselves what relation they have to one another.
> It is plain that they are not living, as in the scene.
> They are obviously marionettes.
> Well, they will not fidget nor complain.

Designed and cut on wood between the years 1907-1915, and every copy personally Hand-printed by the Designer.

HAMLET SERIES

17 Eve
18 Black Girl
19 Hamlet
20 Hamlet
21 Grave Digger
22 Hamlet
23 Ophelia, mad
24 Ophelia, sane
25 Actor
26 Ghost
27 Sentinel
28 Ghost
29 Doubt
30 Laertes

¶

MERCHANT OF VENICE SERIES

31 Young Gobbo
32 Old Gobbo
33 Lorenzo
34 Antonio
35 Shylock
36 Bassanio

¶

37
38 } Suzanne and the Elders
39
40 } Beauty and the Beast
41
42 } Masks
43
44 Hamlet
45 Fear
46 Hunger
47 Lust
48 Moses
49 } The Fencers
50
51 Priest
52 } Roman Actors
53
54 Hamlet and Daeman
55 Group
56 Hekuba
57 Iphigenia
58 Girl with ball
59 Dancing Girl
60 Electra
61 The Jewess
62 Group
63 Cuchulain
64 Girl with stick

few months the total amount of work he did could not have been great. In the previous chapter we have seen the type specimen sheets Morison designed for Cloister and reproduced here are some other "house" jobs which are clearly Morison's work. Their faultless typesetting and presswork is a tribute to Walter Lewis' supervision.

Among Morison's many talents was that of being the best propagandist for a printer's services the trade ever had. This chapter ends with an example of his promotional style in an extract from an article on the Cloister Press written for the September-October 1922 edition of *The Monotype Recorder*:

"Much more is asked of a Printing Press today than ever before. There are many who say unto the printer: *Printing is not what it was*. And again, there are many who say: *Printing is only too much what it was*. So neither the reflective bibliophile nor the farseeing advertiser is satisfied with the general run of book or job or newspaper production.

"But it is hoped that in the Cloister Press the bibliophile, the publisher, and the merchant will find a printer willing and capable of responding to their needs with rare enthusiasm and seasoned knowledge. The Cloister Press is newly established, but, as it is hoped the present pages show, its staff is not new to printing.

"In all its work the Cloister Press seeks to be disciplined by principles of sound design and construction. These principles are based in great part upon the usages of early printers. This is not to say that the Cloister Press policy in this respect is a mere corrupt or even slavish following of the ancients. But it is demonstrable that the fewer types and greater leisure of the early craftsmen resulted in the elucidation of principles of page proportions, margins, etc., which have not been surpassed, though they have been largely discarded in our own generation. William Morris's example, however, has led to a wider recognition of the excellence of the old way. Thus, the placing of the type-area upon the paper, the proportions of margins, the disposal of white space, the degree of leading, and the quality of the impression are all realized to the full of their importance at the Cloister Press. The ever increasing intensity of present-day commercial exploitation and competition demand from the typographer a complete and thorough appreciation of the modern purpose on the one hand, and on the other of the most rapid and inexpensive method of satisfying it. This persistent call for typographical variety and novelty on the part of advertising and publicity specialists has, however, met with a very limited response from the average printer. As a consequence the advertisers' agents have, by means of their own studios and experiments, worked a

The
Distinguished Result
In Printing

1921

THE CLOISTER PRESS · HEATON MERSEY

(38 and 39) In these two title pages both done in 1921 Morison had temporarily abandoned flowered borders for plain but pleasing rule work.

THE CRAFT OF PRINTING

Notes on the History of Type-forms, etc.

LONDON

Printed & Sold

At the PELICAN PRESS, 2 Carmelite Street

A.D. *Mcmxxj*

THE CLOISTER PRESS LTD

Parrs Wood Lane · Heaton Mersey · near Manchester

THE CLOISTER PRESS

WITH COMPLIMENTS

HEATON MERSEY   MANCHESTER

(40 and 41) The letterheading and compliment slip for
the Cloister Press use the newly acquired Garamond
but the ornament and border are far from harmonious.
It is worth comparing them with the Pelican Press items
on page 52.

minor revolution in printing, with the result that the average printer has been generally reduced to the position of a mere mechanical executant. "The Cloister Press is not content with any such servile rôle, and it has, therefore, its own studio and staff of writers. It has thus been made possible for publishers and business men generally to deal direct with an establishment equipped for the production of work in an almost infinite variety of manner. Thus the Cloister Press is not an experiment in revivalism, and it hopes that its imprint will guarantee work which is not merely *antique* or *modern*, but which can be said to be *successful*. The Cloister Press is not, however, indifferent to the achievement of its predecessors, and, since we are all debtors to our fathers, it is not ashamed to acknowledge that it owes much to the example of Aldus, Jenson, the Estiennes, Tory, Jean de Tournes, Plantin, the Elzevirs, our own John Day, Henry Binneman, John Baskerville, and such modern leaders as William Morris, Emery Walker, and Bruce Rogers. While essentially neither a "toy" nor a luxury press, the Cloister Press possesses an enthusiasm for fine work, and it hopes to produce editions which shall hardly fall short of the standard reached by the *Kelmscott*, the *Ashendene*, and the *Doves*, to name the English private presses; the American *Riverside* and *Merrymount* presses; the German *Janus*, *Bremer*, and *Hyperion* presses; and the French *Editions Sirène*, *Pelletan*, and certain issues of MM. Emile Paul, Lucien Vogel, and Ernest Pichon, to name a few commercial ventures. The Cloister Press is therefore not wedded to any one style, ancient or modern, but produces at call the severely plain as well as the ornate 17th century English or 18th century French variety. For the production, indeed, of any kind of "period" printing the Press offers an understanding enthusiasm.

"The Cloister Press, however, does not restrict its interest and capacity to the production of *éditions de luxe* for the *littérateur* and the artist. The Press is equally interested in the problems peculiar to advertisement literature and general commercial printing. The present day is remarkable for the consistent demand for beautiful printing in business. The few presses which have earned a national reputation by the high standard of their craftsmanship have hitherto worked mostly for the connoisseur. But the Cloister Press offers its enthusiasm to the service of commercial affairs, and it is so much interested in sales literature that it offers to write as well as print it. It offers to illustrate sales literature, and is equipped for this also. It designs printing—beautiful printing, but printing, whether of the catalogue, the poster, the leaflet, or the brochure, which is beautiful chiefly in its fitness for the purpose it has to serve."

FELLOWSHIP SERVICES FUND

O N behalf of Miss A. Maude Royden, Dr. Percy Dearmer and the Advisory Council, Mr. Ambrose Pomeroy, J.P., Honorary Treasurer, acknowledges with many thanks your very kind contribution towards the above Fund.

It would give great pleasure if you could attend any of the services.

Afternoons, 3 o'clock.

Evenings, 7 o'clock.

110 Cheapside, E.C.

Date..

Amount received £   *s.*   *d.*

At the Pelican Press

(42) This charming receipt form carries echoes of a nicer, kinder world.

4

WORDS ABOUT FLOWERS

Many typographers have succumbed to the temptation to express their thoughts about that form of ornament known as printers' flowers. Bernard Newdigate gave us this lyrical account of the Aldine leaf with which it all began nearly five centuries ago:

> Nature was the mother of this very beautiful little ornament—a common object of the roadway—a leaf torn by the rough wind from some tree, possibly a willow. Centuries before printing was ever dreamt of, such a leaf fell at the feet of one with a soul for the beautiful, who took it home and drew it and drew it again and again, placing it in various positions and finding a hundred different treatments of the subject, and so discovered

T H E

ALDINE LEAF

1 5 0 1

(43) It's name, what it looks like and the date of it's appearance in print; a Morison tailpiece for the Cloister Press specimen of fleurons.

its possibilities for artistic decorations. In this way it became the basis of most of the designs in Greek and Arabesque pattern books. The architect sculptured it in stone, the lace worker turned it into a dream of delicate beauty, the book binder fashioned it into a tool to stamp his bindings, and in due time the printers cut it in wood and cast it in metal, and it became a stock ornament in every printing office.

With the same intensity of feeling the American typographer W. A. Dwiggins wrote this practical analysis of the Caslon flowers:

Various adaptations of the Aldine Leaf were
developed by the ingenious printers of sixteenth
century France. Lyons craftsmen in par‑
ticular displayed an enthusiasm for arabesque.
Like Aldus, at first they experi‑
mented with small units (circa
1550). At Lyons was first
brought into typography
the triple flower :

(44) A short caption explains the development of the Aldine
leaf. The ornaments below from the Cloister Press specimen
sheet are largely the same as those at the Pelican Press
which Morison and Meynell were at pains to point out were
mostly English.

To a designer's eyes they have taken as individual patterns, an inevitable quality, a finality of right construction that baffles any attempt to change or improve . . . Excellent as single spots, the Caslon flowers multiply their beauties when composed in bands or borders as ornamentation for letterpress. They then become a true flowering of the letter forms—as though particular groups of words had been told off for special ornamental duty and had blossomed at command into intricate, but always typographical patterns. This faculty possessed by the Caslon ornaments of keeping an unmistakable type quality through all their graceful evolution sets them apart from the innumerable offerings of the typefounders' craft as a unique group. . . . From the point of view of the pressman, as practical working types for impressing ink into paper, they may be claimed to be better, so far as English and American designs are concerned, than any type-flowers made since their period. The proportion of printing surface to open paper . . . is excellently adapted for the purposes of clean, sharp impression. Certain ones have elements broken by tint-lines into a clear-printing gray, and it will be observed that this tint is not the gray of copper-plate, but has the weight of solidity of a printing surface backed by metal.

It should be remembered that the material Dwiggins refers to and much more besides had fallen into disuse, and in some cases its place had been taken by forms now despised.

Looking back at the early days of the Pelican Press which he founded in 1916 Francis Meynell wrote: "Bored by the rigid timidity of English 'fine' printing this Press set about reviving the best of the rich printers' ornaments known as 'flowers'. Of these the Pelican Press has made a collection unrivalled in the world; but the influence of its revival has been felt the world over." That claim was completely justified, but as important as their part in reviving the flowers was the way in which Meynell and Morison used them. Writing about the use of ornament in Pelican Press printing Philip James declared that "the taste and versatility shown in their use would alone have earned the Press a place in the history of jobbing printing".[1]

To appreciate the effect on the printing trade, as well as its customers, of this beautiful material it is necessary to compare it with the alternative borders and ornaments offered by the type founders. For example, the firm of Shanks issued many good old style and modern type faces and in 1913 they were responsible for the cutting of the fine Plantin Old Style (which stimulated the later efforts of Monotype), but their decorative material typified the deterioration that had set in during the Victorian era.

[1] *Signature*, No. 12.

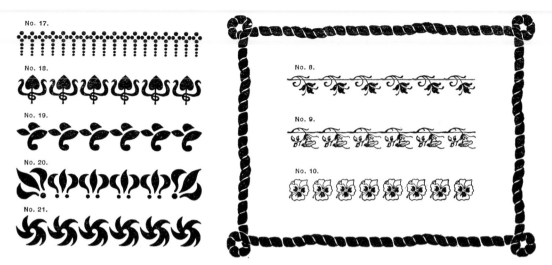

(45) The Victorian ornaments were still in the typefounders catalogues in the nineteen twenties. "Rope Borders", said P. M. Shanks & Sons "give Verisimilitude To an Otherwise Bald and Unconvincing Yarn."

It was not surprising that the flowers caught on thanks largely to Monotype for making them available more cheaply than they could be obtained from other sources. In the middle nineteen-twenties there was hardly a printer in the country who had not bought a few pounds of them from his trade supplier or, if he had the Monotype equipment, cast them for himself. Nor was there a typographer who had not by hook or by crook painted a spray of them on his layouts. It was the heyday of the painted layout.

But the wave of enthusiasm broke itself on the shore of reality. In 1771 Luckombe, writing about a revival of the use of flowers in France, commented

It is to be feared that the Head-pieces, Facs., and Tail-pieces of Flowers will not long continue either in England, France or Germany, considering that the contriving and making them up is attended with considerable trouble and loss of time; and as no allowance is made for this, it will not be strange if but few shall be found who will give instances of their fancy.

And so it was in the nineteen-twenties. Few printers bothered to buy the appropriate corner pieces, often buying single units and ignoring the fact that most of the flowers are designed as pairs. It was common to see a line of ornaments in which one or more were round the wrong way, the moral being that ornaments need the attention of the printer's reader as well as the text. As I write these words I notice a flower-bordered advertisement inserted in *The Bookseller* on behalf of a famous publisher (the same one who wrote asking about the fitness of a printer) in which this happens.

Any fool can put a row of ornaments on a piece of printing, and perhaps Monotype and others contributed to a thoughtless use by making the flowers available in continuous lengths. Another error was to take a design originally and fittingly conceived and cut in 12-point and enlarge it to 18-point or 24-point or even bigger. It was a practice that destroyed the charm of the material and helped in its eventual devaluation. In earlier work too, the flowers were used sparingly, but later work was often spoiled by an excessive weight of ornament.

LVDOVICI CAELII RHO DIGINI LECTIONVM ANTIQVARVM LIBRI XVI

IO. FROB. CANDIDO LECTORI, S. D.

(46) Compare this use of a single flower at the beginning and end of a heading with the title page of the Cloister Press Garamond specimen on page 28.
(47) This attractive eighteenth century use of flower and rule combination has been freely copied by typographers, including Morison.

P O E S I E S

D E S A P H O.

H Y M N E A V É N U S.

It was Morison who introduced a note of warning: "The golden rule with borders, as with other details of the printing art, is that there is no golden rule: no golden rule except that of good taste and good craftsmanship."[1] And again, more explicitly: "A sense of symmetry and design must be brought."[2] His own work shows that he understood Lethaby's advice to architects "not to construct ornament but to ornament construction", but he could and did evolve some splendid borders made up of many units, one of the richest of these being the cover of the specimen book of Monotype Baskerville, printed in light red and gold on dark green.

No account of the use of printers' flowers during the nineteen twenties

[1] *Monotype Recorder*, September–October 1923.
[2] *Monotype Flower Decorations*, 1924.

VOL. XXII

NUMBER 197

THE MONOTYPE RECORDER

SEPTEMBER-OCTOBER

MCMXXIII

ON DECORATION IN PRINTING

FROM the earliest days of the craft, decoration has played an important and interesting part in printing. Elaborate woodcut borders were used at Venice, Florence and other Italian printing centres by renaissance artists. German printers also commissioned similar but heavier decorations for their title pages, and Geofroy Tory brought the graceful Italian semi-floral, semi-architectural method into French books. These wood engravings of somewhat specific application, were followed by simpler strips of pieced-together ornament, which satisfied a more universal purpose. These were in turn succeeded by metal flowers. The 18th century revulsion against ornament gained ground until the fifty years from 1790 to 1840 saw the disuse of all forms of typographical decoration other than fragments of plain rule. So much (or little) for history.

Recently the old ornaments have been revived. William Pickering in the 20's of the nineteenth century recut a number of French woodcut decorations, and the Whittinghams went to the same source for the ornament wherewith they garnished the works printed during the old face revival of the 1840's. But our own day has witnessed a greatly increased interest in smaller units of typographical decoration, and many printers and publishers have welcomed this latest revival. The reason is not far to seek. By the disciplined use of decorative borders and flowers, initials, head and tail pieces, charm and distinction may be given to the page without detracting from the main purpose of print—which is to be read. By these means

(48) Here is Morison's originality with flowers. In the carefully worked out cartouche the inner row of flowers was printed in colour giving a surprising brightness to an already attractive page.

(49) This cover of a Monotype specimen book shows a confident handling of both design and the printing process. The multi-layered border, a combination of rule and ornament was printed in light red on a dark green ground, the title in gold.

JOHN
BASKERVILLE
1757

FOURNIER

A SPECIMEN OF A CLASSIC TYPE

Designed by PIERRE SIMON FOURNIER

circa 1750

Reproduced by

THE LANSTON MONOTYPE CORPORATION LTD

LONDON

(50) In grey and light red on a white ground this flower arrangement was perfect accompaniment for the stylish Fournier.

would be complete without some mention of Frederic Warde whose mastery of the material, sometimes in the manner of Fournier, put him at the head of typographic designers. Morison learned a lot from him and some of Warde's designs have been wrongly attributed to Morison.

Perhaps in a weak moment Francis Meynell wrote this fulsome paragraph:

> But your flowers! They will stand as they are, infinite in their varieties and combinations, and infinitely appropriate. "Come into the garden, Maud!" As flower-borders will sweeten the sight and smell of your garden, so may borders of flowers gladden your pages. Come into the garden; make for yourself fresh poesies. "Gather ye roses while ye may!"

It proved to be almost an epitaph.

By the end of the decade Morison no longer cared for them, and in the general world of typography the flowers had become once more neglected. The worst had happened to them—they were regarded as "stock" borders. This is a fatal attitude, for flowers need even more care than letters if they are to be effectively displayed, and, as Dibdin wrote of types, it is an ill-worker who handles them irreverently.

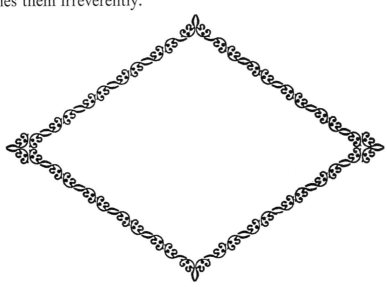

(51 and 52) Some exercises with a single unit, to one of which Morison has added his initials.

5

PAPER AND PATTERN

As the demand for paper increases its quality decreases; the materials used in its making—flax, cotton, hemp, esparto, straw, wood—become progressively scarcer. It is not utterly unlikely in a future age that paper as we know it will be a rare if not a non-existent commodity. It is a prospect that would have dismayed Morison.

From his first days in the trade he took a keen interest in paper, a raw material with a history a thousand years older than printing. In 1915, in an advertisement for the publications of Burns and Oates he wrote in his un-mistakable direct style that a certain book had been "printed on Japon vel-lum—one of the most beautiful papers obtainable". Not everyone would agree with him, least of all a letterpress machine minder, but he had in mind its aesthetic qualities, the subtle shade and pleasant texture.

It was at the Pelican Press that he extended more widely his use of paper. One of the firm's suppliers was G. F. Smith, agents for the Strathmore Paper Company of America, whose papers, though not superior in any way to those of English or European manufacture, were more imaginatively and more persistently promoted at that time. The company had a slogan with which Morison was in full accord: "Paper is part of the picture." For him printing was three-dimensional. What you printed was important, so was what you printed it on. He used the Strathmore papers and also those of Grosvenor Chater, Glastonbury and Greenfield and, later on, Basingwerk. Among the hand-made and mould-made papers he used were Van Gelder and Arches, and he had a preference for laid rather than wove. Morison allowed the deckle to stay on small work and sometimes on bound books, but by the time he wrote *First Principles of Typography* he had come to disapprove of the "ugly, dust-gathering edges" of untrimmed books.

It was of course the use of patterned papers that gave him particular pleasure, described so accurately by Philip James:[1]

In the choice of papers, the remaining ingredient necessary to the printer's art, a similar flair was shown. Here, again, by seeking inspiration in the past a new style of paper covers was introduced. A stock of old italian

[1] *Signature*, No. 12.

53) Morison had a partiality for the pasted on label for books and booklets. The patterned papers he selected were bright but never lurid; top left, a marbled paper in pale blue and dark grey; top right (cover of a book in a series of which he was general editor), light red and yellow on a cream ground; bottom right (cover for a booklet entitled "The Rewards of Better Printing") Cloister Press, black on dull red; centre, light brown on buff; left, old gold on cream. Greatly reduced.)

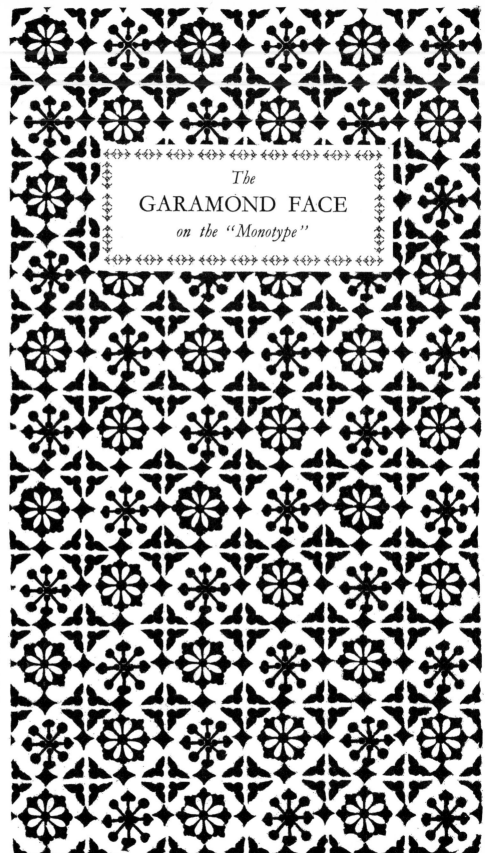

The
GARAMOND FACE
on the "Monotype"

(54) This striking design, printed in red and black on a light brown ground, was popular with Morison who used it on a score of jobs at the Pelican Press and elsewhere.

patterned papers was bought up and used for pamphlets and small books, thus anticipating, if not initiating, the revival of this pleasant material which was so popular throughout the nineteen-twenties.

There were other sources. One of the Pelican's customers was the Dorien Leigh Galleries which as well as selling paintings also imported "precious" papers from China, Korea, Java and Japan. These featherweight materials took Morison's eye, and he used them frequently at the Pelican and indeed took some to Manchester to use at the Cloister Press. A good selection of batik papers was also available at Kettle's shop in New Oxford Street (now in High Holborn) a couple of minutes walk from the British Museum. It was here that Morison bought the paper used for the cover of the Cloister Press booklet *The Rewards of Better Printing*. I am not certain whether this design was used on all copies, for Ernest Ingham showed me at least two copies each with a different pattern used for the cover.

When Morison liked a design he did not hesitate to use it more than once. It did not seem incongrous to him to put Karl Marx and Garamond in identical wrappers, and he used the same design for the covers of a series of booklets for the Trades Union Congress—another of Pelican's oddly assorted customers.

It is apparent from the illustrations in this section that the label was for him the perfect vehicle to carry the title of booklets regardless of their nature. Thanks to giving careful consideration to size and to the type and its arrangement, each one has individuality with no suggestion of repetition. These illustrations also show Morison's preference for muted colours that evoke a world far different to our own in which gloss and varnish are compulsory.

6

THE MAKING OF BOOKS

Printing reaches its highest expression in the book where it comes closest to qualifying as art; this is perhaps why it has attracted so much talent to its practice and continues to do so. But for anyone entering the field of book production today the problems are the same as they were when Theodore Low de Vinne sketched them so vividly about the turn of the century:

> To make a thoroughly good book out of a lot of jumbled manuscript; to select a type appropriate to the subject; to determine its size so that it shall be suitable for the matter in the book; to determine a page so that it shall be in fit proportion to the margin; to correctly determine by graduated size of type the relative importance of extracts, letters, poetry, notes, preface, appendix, index, etc.; to use paper, bindings, and lining papers so that they will be suitable to the print; to space lines neatly, to regulate blanks [whites] properly, so that any reader can see at a glance that the whole book is the work of a disciplined hand and in educated taste, and that proper subordination has been maintained in all the little details, from the space between the words to the margins around the page; these, I think, call for more of skill, more of experience, than are to be shown in the most difficult pieces of ornamental typography. I have said nothing about the difficulty of keeping even colour and exact register, and absolute cleanliness in presswork.

The early printers did not have these problems to the same extent for they regarded their task as an imitative one. They took as their models the manuscript books of their forerunners in book production, the scribes and calligraphers and illuminators who for centuries had devoted themselves to the recording and the development of literature and learning. The type faces of the early printers were copies of the current script hands; in the decoration of the books they printed they copied the rubricators and illuminators, and very often the work of decorating and binding these fifteenth-century printed books was done by the same people who had decorated and bound the hand-written books. It was the ambition of the early printers to make their products indistinguishable from the ones they were to supersede.

Whether it was the spirit of the times in which they lived, or in the nature of the work (mostly religious) that they produced, or the character of the men themselves, the work of the early printers almost invariably achieved a dignity and sometimes a superlative grandeur of form. And this was so even when the type was imperfectly cast, or badly worn and the actual presswork inferior.

But apart from their work they left no guide-lines for those who followed them and, in course of time as the standards of bookwork declined, it became inevitable that certain things had to be learned again. In a similar way, when the intuitive skill of compounding the Wedgwood blue was lost in recent times, it had to be rediscovered by a costly scientific analysis.

Rediscovery was the objective of William Morris when he addressed the Bibliographical Society in London in 1893 on the subject of *The Ideal Book*. Morris's lecture ran to three thousand words and is in the nature of a personal confession of his preferences. But it is no less practical as is shown in this extract relating to the single factor of margins which Morison called the "most important element in typography":

We now come to the position of the page of print on the paper which is a most important point, and one that till quite lately has been wholly misunderstood by modern, and seldom done wrong by ancient printers, or indeed by producers of books of any kind. On this head, I must begin by reminding you that we only occasionally see one page of a book at a time; the two pages making an opening are really the unit of the book; and this was thoroughly understood by the old book producers. I think you will very seldom find a book, produced before the eighteenth century, & which has not been cut down by that enemy of books (& of the human race), the binder, in which this rule is not adhered to: that the binder edge (that which is bound in) must be the smallest member of the margins, the head margin must be larger than this, the fore larger still, and the tail largest of all. I assert that, to the eye of any man who knows what proportion is, this looks satisfactory, & that no other does so look. But the modern printer, as a rule, dumps down his page in what he calls the middle of the paper, which is often not really the middle, as he measures his page from the headline, if he has one, though it is not really part of the page, but a spray of type only faintly staining the head of the paper. Now I go so far as to say that any book in which the page is properly put on the paper, is tolerable to look at, however poor the type may be—always so long as there is no "ornament" which may spoil the whole thing. Whereas any book in which the page is wrongly set on the paper is intolerable to look at, however good the type and ornaments may be.

Ten years later George Bernard Shaw was writing in *The Caxton Magazine* an article entitled "A Criticism of Modern Book Printing":

> Next to evenness and richness of color in the block of letterpress, the most important point in a printed page is the margining. And here the printer is very apt to go wrong. Every printer can understand regularity: few have studied good looks except in living creatures. Consequently they aim at equal margins; and even when they have learnt that an upper margin must be less than a lower one if it is not to look more, they do not always see that it looks well only when it looks less. The medieval manuscript or early printed book, with its very narrow margin at the top and very broad margin at the bottom of the page, with its outer margins broad and its inner ones contracted, so that when the book lies open the two pages seem to make but a single block of letterpress in a single frame, instead of two side by side, has never been improved on and probably never will. But I find it almost impossible to persuade a modern printer to make his top margin small enough; and when I at last succeed, he measures it from the running title instead of from the top line of the page. I saw a book the other day, excellently printed in old-faced type, set solid, on a capital light, clean white crusty paper; yet the page was quite spoiled by an exaggerated top margin, like a masher's collar.

Evidently Morris was talking to the wrong people.

Writing in 1927 on this aspect of typography, Morison was of the opinion "that the mass of books present a tolerable appearance". Today, nearly half a century later, the standard of book production is extremely high and few people would disagree with the suggestion that he had helped to bring about this improvement.

The reader may have supposed from his own preconception of books and printing that the responsibility for the physical appearance of a book rested with either the publisher or the printer. Once upon a time publisher and printer were one (in much the same way that architects were builders), and all printers were book printers—it was the only kind of printing done. But today, with the growth of printing for commerce, few printers are book printers and not all printing craftsmen have been trained in the traditions of book work. In addition to these developments, publishing is now organised as a completely separate business from printing and the publisher as a rule makes the decisions regarding design. Yet, as a writer in the *Monotype Recorder* observed,

anyone who assumed from this that a good book printer today was merely one who took orders from publishers and executed them, as any other manufacturer would, as quickly and as economically as possible, would be betraying a lack of knowledge of the essential qualities and beauties of the printed book, qualities which cannot be assured in advance by the finest types, the most expensive paper, or the most luxurious binding. They are qualities which depend on the actual performance of composing machine and press, or rather upon the training and daily practice of compositors, press-men and other craftsmen under the intelligent and never-ending personal direction of a real printer.

Thus both publisher and printer share the responsibility for the final pro-duction.

The person in a publisher's organisation who has the task of deciding what the books the firm publishes shall look like is called the production manager, although we may look upon him as a designer of books, for this is what he is and would probably prefer to be called. He is the one who must project in his mind's eye the all-important "format". In a large organisation there may be an art director who has a number of designers on his staff.

The book designer may at one time have been a printer with an interest and ability in design generally and particularly in relation to books; he may at one time have called himself a typographer, or a layout man, or even an artist. Like Morison, he may have worked in the publishing business in some other capacity and graduated to the production department. Whatever his background and knowledge of printing, he will most likely have, and needs to have, a more than ordinarily developed perception of "taste" and under-standing of style, as well as considerable executive ability. In the following paragraphs I have tried to give an outline of a Morisonian approach to rational book design.

The first thing that has to be decided in the making of a book is its size. The greatest of the book designer's skills is called upon for the early stages of the job. The size of a book cannot be settled only by a consideration of the length of the manuscript, as the number of words influences the size of the page to a certain extent. For instance, to choose a comparatively small page-size for a very long manuscript and to use an average size of type and paper of average thickness would result in a book squat and awkward to hold. If, however, a small page-size could not be avoided then the type size must also be small. The book designer has three dimensions to play with: height, width and thickness, and when the first two are pre-determined the third can be controlled by the number of words on a page and by the thickness or thinness of the paper used.

If the reader will familiarise himself with the parts of a book he will under-stand quite readily the typographer's job in relation to his needs. Take the page, which is the basic unit of the book. Here is a rectangle of words, of "print" or type, surrounded by plain paper—the margins, called respectively the "back" (that is, the one in the centre of the book), the "head", the "fore-edge", and the "tail" margins. The other items on the page are the chapter title or a running headline and the number of the page. Of all the hundreds of pages of books you have looked at before, you may probably never have been conscious of this construction. The positioning of this area of words on the paper is responsible for this unconscious acceptance. If the back margin were less you might find that your eye occasionally jumped across to read a word on the opposite page and so interrupt reading. If the tail or fore-edge margins were less you might find your thumbs at times obscuring words at the ends of lines. The area of words on the paper must appear to be perfectly at rest where it is; and you *are* conscious of it when by accident an imperfect sheet has got bound into the book with different head and tail margins facing one another.

In reading a book the eyes must be moved from left to right and then slightly faster from right to left many thousands of times. The fact that this can be done effortlessly, involuntarily almost, is due to the selection of the length of line in relation to the size of type or number of words in a line. The eye can follow a line containing about ten or twelve words, disconnect at the right-hand end of the line and then quite easily light upon the first word at the left-hand end of the line immediately following. But imagine a line two or three times the length of this one you are reading now and containing about twenty or thirty words, and consider the difficulty that would continually be experienced in accurately finding the beginning of the right line of reading. Could one easily read a book of a hundred thousand words if it were printed in that style? Too few words in a line equally undesirable because it requires a too frequent disconnecting of the eye from line to line—a race with the words and the reader ahead of the words.

The margins, and the length of line or number of words in a line, are two of the principal considerations of the page. On the size of the page depends the size of the type that can be used without the readers becoming unduly aware of its being relatively larger or smaller. The reader will automatically adjust the distance from his eye at which he can read in comfort.

Refinements in the actual setting of the type which make for ease of reading are evenness of the space between the words in a line which should be as con-sistent as possible from line to line; and occasionally, the spacing between the lines which eases the act of disconnecting the eye from the end of one line to the beginning of the next.

The designer of books usually arrives at a common-sense decision by what is almost second nature to him in the choosing of a page-size in relation to length of manuscript, but there are times when he has need of a rare sense to satisfy the special and individual claims of both author and reader in the right format for a particular manuscript.

"Format" then means, almost at one and the same time, page-size in relation to the number of words (which, with paper, determines the thickness of the book), and the suitability, the appropriateness, of this format to the subject matter.

There are certain publishing conventions that are quite logical, such as that which results in most novels being originally of a uniform size from whatever firm they are issued. That there is so much variety in this restricted format is a tribute to the production department's resourcefulness.

Next comes the choice of type and the decision of the size of the chosen design. Whatever else in the mechanics of book production the ordinary reader may claim, or be presumed, to be totally unaware of, it is certain that he knows that there are differences in the styles of printed letters. It is supremely important to the book designer.

"Of the raw materials which go to the making of a fine book" wrote Morison,[1] "most important is the form of its letter." It was a subject he looked at from two points of view—the design of the type and how it was used. When Morison first became interested in printing the private press movement was still enjoying the afterglow of its fame, and although he acknowledged the movement's aims and applauded its overall achievements he was not enamoured of some of the type faces it threw up.

The Venetian model of Jenson and his contemporaries dominated the private press type and Morison looked with considerable distaste at the most celebrated of them.

For example, he described William Morris's Golden type as having an "ugly appearance". "Pretentious and notorious failures" was the sweeping dismissal of the faces designed for the Essex House, Eragny, Kings and Vale Presses, and he went on to say that "the cause of fine printing has suffered much from a vulgar craze for queer proprietary styles". The type faces still most in use in book printing in the early part of this century he held to be "stiff, thin, regimental and savourless".

It was this dissatisfaction with most of the types in use when he entered the printing industry that caused Morison to look at the past in a search for the great types that he was subsequently responsible for making once again available to the trade through the medium of the Monotype composing

[1] *On Type Faces.* (Medici Society.)

despoylled hym of all other thynges. And he, his wyf, and children
thanked god and fledde awey by nyght al naked, and by cause they
doubted shame they fledde in to Egypte. And alle his grete posses,
sion cam to nought by rauayne of wycked peple. Thenne the kynge
and alle the Senatours sorowed moche for the maister of the chyual,
rye whiche was so noble, by cause they myght here no tydynges of
hym. ℂ And as they wente they approched the see, and fonde a
shippe and entryd in to hit for to passe, and the maistre of the shyp
saw the wyf of Eustace was ryght fayre, and desyred moche for to

A NEW PROPOSAL MADE BY THE ESSEX HOUSE PRESS TO ITS PATRONS & SUBSCRIBERS.

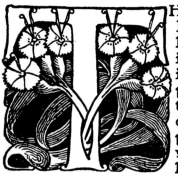

HE ESSEX
House Press
has pleasure
in announc,
ing that it is
prepared to
take special
orders from
private indi,
viduals for
hand print,
ing of the finest sort.
The work of the Press is well enough
known to justify it in offering some,
thing that shall have a character and
individuality of its own and not be in
competition with Trade work. More,
over it is only proposed to do work
that shall be limited in number of

(55, 56, 57 and 58) Some types of the Private
Presses. Above, Morris's Golden type; left, the
Essex House Press type; below right, the Brook
type of the Eragny Press; bottom, the Riccardi
type designed by Herbert P. Horne for the Medici
Society.

❧ THE ERAGNY PRESS, THE BROOK, HAMMERSMITH, LONDON, W. (No. 10). NOW READY.

❧ One hundred and seventy,five
copies have been printed in red &
black throughout with the «Brook»
type on «Arches» linen hand,made
paper with the Eragny Press water,
mark. Of these, one hundred and
fifty are for sale in England and
America at forty shillings net.

illuminator and calligrapher. The form of printing types then underwent
slight modification, and there was produced the first of a new variety character
ized by short bracketed serifs to the capitals, themselves somewhat narrowe
than those used by the Venetians, and, most important, the addition to the roma
of a cursive face for companion use. In other words Garamond evolved the firs
face in which roman and italic were treated as constituents of one fount. Hithe
to italic (which had been invented by Aldus in 1501) had been a fount in itsel
It was used for the entire text of the work and with it were used roman capital
In Garamond's hands the italic caps first appeared, and we are at once in th

machine. That story has been told elsewhere—what interests us here is Morison's own book work.

One book is sufficient to illustrate Morison's time with the Catholic publishing firm of Burns and Oates, the poems of one of the most controversial members of the faith in his day, G. K. Chesterton, published in 1915. Morison was fortunate in going to a publisher who employed two of the most competent book printers of the day, Charles Jacobi and Bernard Newdigate who represented The Chiswick Press and The Arden Press respectively. With the high standard of these men to inspire them it was not difficult for the young Morison and Francis Meynell, who was also at Burns and Oates, to produce sound work. They did this and more by introducing the printer's flowers to which they had become attracted. The title page of the Chesterton book is a run-of-the-mill job with the basic elements that could well have been the copy set for the City and Guild examination in compositor's work. But several factors lift the book well above the ordinary. First of all there are the initials specially cut by Eric Gill and one of the earliest examples of his Roman to be seen in print. It is interesting to report in passing that these initials, presumably cut on wood "because the photographic line-block is essentially an inferior article"[1], must have been taken great care of by The Chiswick Press storekeeper for they appear six years later in a leaflet printed by The Pelican Press. The other distinctive feature of the book is the binding; red buckram with a border of flowers taken right to the edge, with a further group of flowers under the title, all blocked in gold. The top edge is gilt, with the foredge and tail uncut giving it a total effect of a sixteenth-century breviary. The size was Pott octavo, a format that has virtually disappeared from use. After nearly sixty years since it was published the production has lost none of its charm. (This copy, bought in a secondhand bookshop recently, bears the signature of G. D. H. Cole on the fly leaf.) When it was reprinted in the twenties the paper substance was reduced, the tissue protecting the frontispiece portrait was dispensed with and blind blocking replaced gold for the border on the front of the binding, all perhaps indications of the changes being forced on publishers by economics. The Chesterton is fairly representative of the Burns and Oates style of production which often brought praise from reviewers. Although Morison and Meynell frequently worked there as a team, Mr Tom Burns is certain on reflection that "Morison must have done a good deal of designing singlehanded."

Four grim years separate the volume of Chesterton's poems from *Living Temples* a book of meditations by Bede Jarrett, the first book indisputably Morison's own work. Again the size is Pott octavo. The title page is plain

[1] *Autobiography*. Eric Gill. (Jonathan Cape.)

G. K. Chesterton
From a Photograph by Hector Murchison

POEMS
BY GILBERT KEITH CHESTERTON

BURNS & OATES, LTD.
28 ORCHARD STREET
LONDON, W.
1915

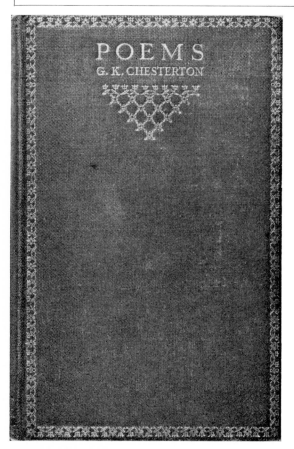

THE NEW FREETHINKER

JOHN Grubby, who was short and stout
   And troubled with religious doubt,
   Refused about the age of three
To sit upon the curate's knee;
(For so the eternal strife must rage
Between the spirit of the age
And Dogma, which, as is well known,
Does simply hate to be outgrown).
Grubby, the young idea that shoots,
Outgrew the ages like old boots;
While still, to all appearance, small,
Would have no Miracles at all;
And just before the age of ten
Firmly refused Free Will to men.
The altars reeled, the heavens shook,
Just as he read of in the book;
Flung from his house went forth the youth
Alone with tempests and the Truth,
Up to the distant city and dim
Where his papa had bought for him
A partnership in Chepe and Deer
Worth, say, twelve hundred pounds a year.

98

(59, 60 and 61) After sixty years the gold is still bright on the buckram binding of this volume of Chesterton's poems, the first book Morison and Meynell produced together at Burns and Oates and an early, brave use of the revived flowers.

I am making every effort in my power to secure the greater glory and happiness and peace and spiritual advancement of that nation to which I have pledged myself. Hence there can be no limit other than faith and conscience to be set to loyalty, even though true loyalty may seem at times not to pay. It is far better to suffer through loyalty than to gain by disloyalty, though loyalty may sometimes mean opposition to popular favour. This point may be noted in the oath that the Greek boy took when he reached manhood: "I will do battle for our altars and our homes, whether aided or un-aided. I will leave our country not less but greater and nobler than she was entrusted to me. I will reverently obey the citizens who shall act as judges. I will obey the laws which have been ordained and which in time to come shall be ordained by the national will."

Honour

HONOUR is the basis of all Christian life; it is the union in one word of all the virtues that Our Lord came to preach; it is the establishment of a perfect code of moral law upheld simply by generosity. To be honourable requires an immense amount of

94

---

218 EPISTOLÆ

Ortuinum Gratium, in quo utique codiculo feu li-bello, ficut talis dederit mihi intelligendum, con-tinentur omnes literulæ ad veftram dignitatem hinc-inde deftinatæ charitative & fraternaliter à reftris amicis & notis, etiam pofueritis meum epiftolium intus, & valde miratorie ftupefactus fuerim, quòd dignamini me tantifper honore fefquipedali, & fa-citis mihi æternalem famam, quapropter habueritis fcire, quatenus voluerim vobis gratiam referre, in quantum potuero, etiam fciveritis, qualiter ftuduero hic per totum in poefeos artificiolo, & ergo fuerim aliter ftilatus quàm prius. Valete fefquipedaliter. Da-tum Romæ.

Frater Georgius Bleck M. Ortuino Gratio.

HUMILEM orationem meam, cum ea quæ decet fubjectione Magifter: Qnia vos mi-fiftis mihi huc librum Ioa. Pfefferkorn, qui eft prætitulatus: Defenfio Ioan. Pfefferkorn contra famofas, quem utique petiviftis, oftendi omnibus Magiftris noftris per totam Parrhifiam, & fimiliter de noftro ordine Theologis, qui unanimiter dixerunt: Ecce Almania habet notabiles Theologos: Si unus fimplex fcribit talia, quid deberent facere docti & promoti? & unus interrogavit me, an etiam Prin-cipes in Almania faciunt magnam reverentiam, Joan-ni Pfefferkorn? Refpondi, quod pro parte non. Et qualiter ipfe eft verus & dilectus follicitator Impe-ratoris, ad procurandum negotium de libris Judæo-rum & augmentum fidei Chriftianæ. Et quòd Epi-fcopus Moguntinenfis piæ memoriæ, defunctus jam, folebat

---

(62 and 63) A page from "Living Temples" published by Burns, Oates and Washbourne and according to the imprint "printed by Stanley Morison at the Pelican Press" which seems to suggest that he was proud of it. It is an utterly traditional exercise but lacks perhaps some of the ease of the eighteenth century page on the right.

but strong, and although the device is a trifle too large it gives a liveliness to the page. Why Morison chose the Italian type face for the text when he did not particularly care for it and seldom used a Venetian letter, is not easy to understand. It is clear and legible but the page is somehow wooden, lacking the sureness of the seventeenth-century book which has an almost identical make-up.

The remainder of the illustrations in this section show Morison's handling of bookwork in the period after leaving the Pelican Press when he worked for a number of publishers. First of all let us look at some title pages. "The

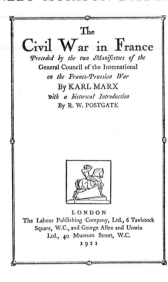

(64, 65, 66, 67 and 68) Morison was largely committed to the tapered style of display for his early title pages. In the Shelley there is a hint of the style he formulated for Gollancz, where there is no attempt to make a pattern but to let each line make what it will although giving much more thought to the preparation of the wording.

JULIUS MEIER-GRAEFE
AUTHOR OF VINCENT VAN GOGH, &c.

DEGAS

RENDERED INTO ENGLISH
BY J. HOLROYD-REECE
WITH MORE THAN
ONE HUNDRED
PLATES

LONDON: ERNEST BENN, LIMITED
8 BOUVERIE STREET E.C.
1923

THE COMPLETE WORKS OF
PERCY BYSSHE SHELLEY
NEWLY EDITED BY ROGER INGPEN AND WALTER E. PECK
IN TEN VOLUMES

POEMS: VOLUMES I–II–III–IV

VOLUME I

POEMS

PUBLISHED FOR
THE JULIAN EDITIONS
in LONDON by ERNEST BENN LIMITED and in
NEW YORK by CHARLES SCRIBNER'S SONS
1927

history of printing is in large measure the history of the title page",[1] he wrote, an observation he qualified by the suggestion that it was possible "to exaggerate the invention and function of the title-page".[2] In some of his first title pages Morison strained to achieve the tapered effect seen at its best in sixteenth-century French book printing. To succeed in this style it is helpful to have a fair amount of copy to play with so that the shape is apparent at first glance. In the title page for *The Civil War in France* the intended design is clear, but in the title page of *Swann's Way* it is hardly noticeable.

The most imposing book Morison produced in 1923 for Benn was Julius Meier-Greafe's enthralling life of the impressionist painter Degas. "By earlier standards the presswork of today's book printing would be judged to be suffering from a deficiency of ink" wrote Savage in the middle of the nineteenth century. Others echoed his complaint in the 1890's, and it is one that could be made today. But not of the Degas, a substantial medium quarto, well-inked with firm impression on unbleached Arnold, bound in leather to give the authoritative feel of the books of the great printers. The layout of the title page again is tapered but the stability is undermined by the use of italic, especially at the foot. Each text page carries instead of a running headline the same rule and ornament (a combination Morison used again and again) as on the first page, but it seems somehow unobtrusive and certainly does not merit William Morris's description of the running headline as an excrescence.

About this time Morison became involved with Robert Bridges, one of the fruits of this association being the production of a small collection of Bridges' poems under the title of *The Tapestry*. In his youth Bridges had written in one of his short poems:

> I love all beauteous things,
> I seek and adore them;
> God hath no better praise,
> And man in his hasty days
> Is honoured for them.
>
> I too will something make
> And joy in the making.

Morison's fond attention to *The Tapestry* showed that he too cared for "beauteous things". The most important thing about it is the Arrighi type, the printer's note referring to "our new cursive type" although Frederick Warde alone is usually credited with its design. The book is a cut-down royal octavo

---

[1] *First Principles of Typography*, Cambridge University Press.
[2] *The English Newspaper*, Cambridge University Press.

ON TYPE FACES

EXAMPLES OF THE USE OF TYPE FOR THE
PRINTING OF BOOKS: WITH AN INTRO-
DUCTORY ESSAY & NOTES BY STANLEY
MORISON. PUBLISHED JOINTLY BY
THE MEDICI SOCIETY OF SEVEN
GRAFTON ST. LONDON W.
AND THE FLEURON
WESTMINSTER
MCMXXIII

(69) The title page of "On Type Faces" is a good example of the bad habit of forcing words into a preconceived shape, in this case the all too familiar one in printing of the inverted pyramid, which Morison later condemned. By incorporating the publisher's imprint with the subtitle it no longer looks like what the reader expects a title page to look like.

D E G A S

¶ CHAPTER I

THE OLD MAN wore a wide circular cloak, rather shabby but scrupulously clean. He used to take a tram every day from Montmartre to some quarter of Paris. There he would descend and enter another car. He did not care where he went. The old man sat motionless. When the conductor appeared, he pulled out his sous rather hastily but without looking. He did not read in the tram as the others did; he looked straight over the head of whoever happened to sit opposite to him. He never said a word to anyone and no one greeted him.

"Rum chap!" said the conductor to his colleague at the terminus. In French there are many expressions to describe queer people, and tram conductors have a variety of their own.

In the afternoon his cloaked figure descended the Rue Lafitte from Notre Dame de Lorette. He had known every stone in the street for the last half-century. The old man walked slowly, guiding his cloak carefully through the throng of people, and seemed more intent than others upon evading contact with his fellows; for this very reason, he was less successful than the bolder spirits who slipped in and out with fish-like agility. Every now and again he stood still, swaying a little. He was a curious spectacle among the fleet-footed passers-by, who appeared to spend most of their time in the streets. He looked almost as though his centre of gravity was stationary while his limbs moved onwards. He carried his head immobile through the crowd. His eyes were fixed, looking up a little, like those of a blind man. Sometimes his expression became rigid and his whole appearance suggested the mysterious giants, whose motionless masks are borne aloft on high poles, covered with enormous flowing mantles, during Carnival in Spain.

He was a stranger, although everyone knew him, and although he had fingered each door-handle in the Rue Lafitte a hundred times. Impenetrability was the cloak he wore. When he entered a house everyone moved shyly to one side, while his host advanced somewhat uneasily to offer him a respectful welcome. Behind the counters in shops, the assistants put their heads together and in whispers exhausted the range of the French vocabulary for "Rum

(70) The quarto page poses one of the hardest problems to the book designer. What size of type? What length of line? Or would double column be better? In the "Degas" the line may be just a little too long but the type was well placed on the page and the general effect was pleasing. The rule and ornament at the head, a combination Morison often employed, was repeated on every page.

¶ ST. PETER

In Kensington Gardens this morning at seven
we met Saint Peter—if you please
shut out (he let us know) from heaven,
because he'd dropped or lost his keys.

What was he doing? You'll hardly credit
our tale. He'd launched the largest yacht
the Round Pond ever saw, and said it
was one he'd found there on the spot.

But Ann knew better. He had found it
where no winds ruffle sails—thought she—
and how could they, who stood around it,
sail it if there was no more sea?

And "look!" Ann said. I thought she beckoned
to someone—but no doubt the trees
misled us both, or else that second
Saint Peter must have found the keys.

KENSINGTON
GARDENS

by

HUMBERT WOLFE

ERNEST BENN LTD.
8 Bouverie Street, E.C.
1924

(71) The Humbert Wolfe poems are another of the very impressive productions along with the Shelley and the Degas done for Benn. The title page with its sparing but novel use of flowers is lifted out of the ordinary.

and as it sucketh swelleth, til it burst its case
and thrusting its roots downward and spreading them wide
taketh tenure of the soil, and from ev'ry raindrop
on its dribbling passage to replenish the springs
plundereth the freighted salt, while it pricketh upright   50
with its flagstaff o'erhead for a place in the sun,
anon to disengage buds that in tender leaves
unfolding may inhale provender of the ambient air:
and, tentacles or tendrils, they search not blindly
but each one headeth straightly for its readiest prey;
and haply, if the seed be faln in a place of darkness
roof'd in by men—if ther should be any ray or gleam
how faint soe'er, 'twil crane and reach its pallid stalk
into the crevice, pushing ev'n to disrupt the stones.

   'Tis of such absolute selfhood that it knoweth not   60
parent nor offspring, and will abuse advantage
of primogeniture, with long luxuriant boughs
crowding in vain-glory to overshadow and quell
its younger brethren; while, as for its own children
that, cradled on its branches, fell from its fruitage,
'twil choke them when they strive to draw life at its feet.

   Look now upon a child of man when born to light,
how otherwise than a plant sucketh he and clutcheth?
how with his first life-breath he clarioneth for food!
craving as the blind fledgelings in a thrush's nest   70
that perk their naked necks, stiff as a chimney-stack,
food-funnels, like as hoppers in a corn-mill gaping
for what supply the feeder may shovel in their throats.
How differeth the new-born child from plant or fledgeling?
   Among low organisms some are call'd animal

[31]

(72) The problems of the quarto page are more readily solved when setting
verse and there is little need for restraint in the size of type to be used. A
page from Robert Bridges's masterpiece "The Testament of Beauty" which
the poet laureate dedicated to King George the Fifth.

THE TAPESTRY

Poems

by

Robert Bridges

London
Privately Printed
Mcmxxv

(73) The Tapestry
was frankly preci-
ous although this
attenuated title
page is saved by
a daring use of
ornament to give
wings to the au-
thor's name.

barely a quarter of an inch thick with marbled boards, and has the title on a spine label only. For those interested in the perennial debate as to whether a title should read up or down the spine, this one read up as in many other instances of Morison's work. Beatrice Warde, on the other hand, expressed the view (in a letter to the author) that titles that read up the spine "send a shiver down mine".

The Japanese vellum used for the text is brittle and has a rather poor opacity, but for all this *The Tapestry* has an exquisite overall character. The imprint states that it was printed by "F. W. and S. M." but Ernest Ingham assures me that it was he and Morison who printed the sheets in the evening when the technical staff at the Fanfare Press had gone home. None of this mattered to the regular pressman whose only comment after these nocturnal operations was to ask why he had to wash up the rollers every morning.

Another work of Bridges that Morison designed was the 1929 edition of *The Testament of Beauty*. Its noble language is well displayed on a demy quarto page, set in 16-point Bembo. One looks with dismay at the title page, a quite inadequate announcement of what is to follow.

In the nineteen twenties Benn was one of the most adventurous publishing houses in London, using some of the best book printers in the country and having on its staff excellent typographers such as Charles Hughes and Bernard Glemser. In 1923 the firm produced *The Player's Shakespeare*, possibly the most beautiful editions of Shakespeare produced in the twentieth century. It was printed at the Shakespeare Head Press under the direction of Newdigate and Frank Sidgwick described it as "matchless". With Harley Granville-Barker, famous for his Prefaces as textual editor and Albert Rutherston as art director, it was illustrated by contemporary artists among whom were Thomas Lowinsky, Paul Nash, Charles Ricketts and Norman Wilkinson. Morison was a spectator at this feast and it gave him an appetite for comparable tasks.

The opportunity occurred a year or so later with a new edition of the complete works of Shelley, which Roger Inkpen and Walter Peck had been working on for so long and with such skill and dedication. In a way the problem of how to present this work was much more complicated that in the case of a Shakespeare where the great bulk of text setting is in one style. The Shelley has poems, plays, and prose works of uneven extent, essays, letters and so on. Again *The Player's Shakespeare* was obviously intended for the collector while the Shelley must make its way as a trade edition acceptable to the librarian, and the general reader as well as the collector. The organisation of a vast amount of material into a reasonable number of volumes of convenient bulk requires the kind of planning described earlier, while to control the

A REVIEW OF
RECENT TYPOGRAPHY
IN ENGLAND · THE UNITED STATES
FRANCE & GERMANY

by

STANLEY MORISON

With sixteen illustrations

LONDON
THE FLEURON LIMITED
1927

(74) This title page
another of his
books is in line
his latter statem
about capitals
small capitals an
size (not more
twice the size of
text) though her
has gone to the
extreme.

DINNERS
LONG AND SHORT
by
A. H. ADAIR

WITH AN INTRODUCTION
by
X. MARCEL BOULESTIN

AND A PORTRAIT
by
MARIE LAURENCIN

LONDON
VICTOR GOLLANCZ LTD
14 Henrietta Street Covent Garden
1928

(75) One of the early title pages for Gollancz in which the precise, controlled arrangement which was to last for many years is developing. It is worth comparing with the Chesterton poems (page 84) in which the elements are the same.

typographical detail and the binding design to produce a result in the category of fine printing called for the highest talent. Typographically the Shelley is austere, set in Baskerville, like the poet, a product of the age of elegance. Tho only ornament is on the spine label where flowers have been arranged with some "cunning", to use a word habitually chosen by Morison to describe the things that pleased him. It is a well-known fact that when books have a special literary or typographic distinction they acquire a reputation and disappear almost as soon as they are published, rarely turning up even in the most celebrated antiquarian booksellers' catalogues. The Julian editions enjoyed that sort of fame.

Morison is at his most contrary and controversial in his comments on the design of the title page, arbitrarily stating what size of types to be used for the title of the book, what should be in capitals and how they should be set. In *First Principles of Typography* he describes the practice of printers in the past

MARTIN ARMSTRONG

═══

THE FIERY DIVE

AND

OTHER STORIES

═══

LONDON
VICTOR GOLLANCZ LTD
14 Henrietta Street Covent Garden
1929

ERNEST GEORGE

BELLE

A PLAY

══

LONDON
VICTOR GOLLANCZ LTD
14 Henrietta Street Covent Garden
1929

(76 and 77) Typical Gollancz title pages though some of them were the "bleak affairs" he disliked. A special narrow format (7¼ ins. by 4¼ ins.) was devised for the plays.

to use larger sizes, black letters and to include their device, and he declares that now these have vanished, "the contemporary title page is generally a bleak affair, exhibiting in nine out of ten cases such a space between the title and the imprint of the printer-publisher, that the blank tends to be the strongest feature of the page." This is one of the details he had to reckon with in evolving a style of production for Gollancz which it is now worth while looking at as a whole.

Morison cut through the pretentiousness of the type fanciers, who make so much of choosing what they think are suitable faces for various texts or subjects, by specifying one type face for the whole Gollancz productions—Baskerville.

Morison had already noted, and later wrote, that Baskerville is "a type

CATALOGUE OF

I

TYPEFOUNDERS' SPECIMENS

II

BOOKS PRINTED IN FOUNTS OF HISTORIC IMPORTANCE

III

WORKS ON TYPEFOUNDING PRINTING & BIBLIOGRAPHY

OFFERED FOR SALE

BIRRELL & GARNETT, LTD

Booksellers

30, Gerrard Street, Soho

LONDON

1928

(78) Morison expressed his satisfaction for this title page. Some typographers would have felt uncomfortable about mixing the Fry Baskerville with the Monotype cutting.

obstacle was a woman and the irresistible force only a man, he had to find a way out. " Go out and buy a ring and a licence," he said. And within a week Miss Townshend found herself a married woman ; and Shaw was a married man. When the Webbs returned from their circumnavigation of the globe they found the pair on Hindhead completely settled. Shaw, no longer a free lance, took on the appearance by which this generation knows him ; that of a country gentleman up in town. And he became an armchair Socialist. The dock gates, the parks, the suburban commons, the street corner pitches, the market squares, and the town halls had seen the last of him ; and the Sunday At Home became a Shavian institution.

I, in my innocence, believed that people married either for love or money. Shaw would not allow that he had married for either. " We married," he said, " because we had become indispensable to one another." And that appears to be the plain truth.

He was still very ill when they were married by the West Strand registrar, still on crutches and wearing a jacket which, he swears, his crutches had worn to rags in the armpits.

Graham Wallas and Henry Salt acted as witnesses.

" In honour of the occasion they were dressed in their best clothes," Shaw continued, as I remember his relating the incident. " The registrar never imagined I could possibly be the bridegroom ; he took me for the inevitable beggar who completes all wedding processions. Wallas, who was over six feet tall, seemed to the registrar to be the hero of the occasion, and he was calmly proceeding to marry him to my betrothed when Wallas, thinking the formula rather strong for a witness, hesitated at the last minute and left the prize to me."

gun-boats, and half a dozen river steamers, and a dozen barges. Kut is twenty miles up-stream. Five miles from it, nearer us, at Es-sinn, the Turkish army is astride the Tigris, which here runs roughly west to east. Nur-ud-din's position is one of great strength. His right rests on a high irrigation cut, heavily entrenched and wired. A ferry connects this southern position with another system of trenches in the Horse-Shoe Marsh, north of the river. Then there are more trenches, another big marsh (the Suwada) and finally another mile of trenches more lightly fortified. Along this line, from south to north, Nur-ud-din is supposed to have five thousand regular and four thousand irregular troops, and eighteen guns. Another three thousand men are in reserve, nearer Kut, and on the Tigris he has six steamers, three launches, a dozen barges. The country is as flat as a pancake, except for the irrigation cuts and the marshes.

The Turks dig like moles. A frontal attack would be fatal in this open ground against such a difficult position.

Alphonso is full of confidence, however. He has telegraphed to Basra in his flippant way, to say that now that Nur-ud-din is within punching distance, he'll put him out for the count. We have pitched camp on the right bank of the river at Sunnayat, in order to make Nur-ud-din think that we mean to attack on that side, and we shall make a demonstration there, on the day

173

(79 and 80) These two pages from demy octavo books set in the same size type, show the adaptability of Baskerville. By differing length of line, page depth and margins, the long Frank Harris manuscript was contained within 400 pages and the Yeats Brown, little more than half its length, was pushed out to nearly 300 pages. Yet both pages are easy to read and both books had good double page openings.

(81 and 82) These two pages must be regarded as experiments and that for "The Testament of Beauty" as a failure, with too much matter compressed into a small area (Original demy quarto.) "Gunman" is an attempt at modernity that did not succeed.

ROBERT BRIDGES

THE TESTAMENT OF BEAUTY
A POEM IN FOUR BOOKS

Oxford
AT THE CLARENDON PRESS·
1929

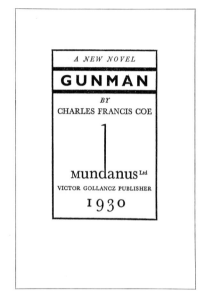

to which leading is invariably an advantage",[1] and he could have gone on to say that another of its merits is its utility in the matter of leading. This is apparent in the pages of two books from the first years of Gollancz. It is particularly worth noting how the eleven point size has been given different leading quite satisfactorily. These pages also show how the traditional rules for page margins can be worked out for different type areas on the same page size with no feeling of rigidity. Two other details are the running head incorporating the page number in one case or putting it at the foot to increase the apparent depth of the page. To start chapters Morison chose to use a small upstanding initial followed by lower case. The disadvantage of this method is that it involves hand justification and unless scrupulously done there is the risk that the initial will not align perfectly at the foot with the following letters. It has the advantage of giving emphasis to the chapter opening while avoiding

[1] *First Principles of Typography.* (Cambridge University Press.)

(83) It was with the binding of the Gollancz books that Morison demonstrated his understanding of book design and rounded off his contribution. By taking the title and publisher's imprint to the extreme head and foot respectively the spine is revealed as an organic part of the book. Using gold blocking and various coloured inks, almost exclusively on black cloth, he established an outstanding house style.

the question of how many words should be in capitals, and eliminating the unsightly gaps left around dropped initials when the type is not closely fitted at the right and below the initial letter. With the title page Morison had to be content with the amount of copy provided by the title and author's name. When there was additional matter that helped to increase the depth he occasionally added a sparkle to the page with thick and thin cut-off rules, a device imported from the newspaper, and by adding the address to the publisher's name he gave some weight to the foot of the page.

Nicolas Barker calls Morison's specification "fool-proof book design"[1], but I reject this phrase entirely as doing justice to neither Morison nor the printing trade craftsmen who made such a success of it. Finally, to the binding, where by standardising a black cloth and a sans serif lettering akin to Gill, he achieved an effect both clear and elegant. Never before had all the elements of bookmaking, incorporating such a high degree of mechanical means, been put together so skilfully in the making of a style for a commercial publisher. The excellent condition of the volumes shown in the photograph, all produced over forty years ago and bought recently in secondhand bookshops after passing through several owners, is evidence that as well as being well-designed they were well-made. I regard the books designed by Morison years later as perfect examples of polished period reproductions, lacking the vitality of his early empirical approach.

Over the greater part of this period, and which must be mentioned, there was his work on the seven volumes of *The Fleuron*. To credit anyone with the design would be to risk many inaccuracies and besides, with the combined resources of The Curwen Press and The Cambridge University Press the naming of a typographer would be superfluous. One detail worth noting is the binding of volume five which has the same look as the spines of Gollancz books he was experimenting with at the time.

[1] *Stanley Morison*, Nicolas Barker. (Macmillan.)

7

GOLLANCZ DAYS

At some point in time in the last century the book dust wrapper ceased to have a purely utilitarian role and found a new one, becoming an advertisement for the book at the point of sale.

In the year that Victor Gollancz ended his association with the publisher Benn and started up in business on his own, Morison wrote in *A Review of Recent Typography*: "Sales copy is designed to be read by the unwilling, and therefore he needs to be dragged into perusal by every sort of typographical seduction." It could well have been a formula for the jackets that gave instant recognition to the Gollancz books that began to appear in booksellers' windows in the late nineteen-twenties and have indeed been there ever since in increasing numbers.

It is a mistake to think of the Gollancz jackets as a creation of Morison alone. They were essentially the joint product of Gollancz, the brilliant copy-writer, and Morison who invented a way of typographically articulating that copy, with the aim of giving every word the utmost chance of being read. They were also an extension of a man's personality. In conversation Gollancz did not mince his words, he shot them out loud and clear to his listeners, whether they were standing by his side, downstairs or on the telephone a hundred miles away. V. G. was seldom misunderstood, and Morison under-stood perfectly. He played with the words as if they were toys, arranged them distractingly, disturbingly, dangerously almost, on the yellow ground, in a conscious effort to catch the reader's roving eye.

There was a third man involved in the operation, Ernest Ingham, who came down to London from The Cloister Press and was manager of the Fanfare Press, part of the London Press Exchange in St. Martin's Lane. It was about this time that Ingham went to Germany in the wake of Morison and visited the leading German typefounders, Klingspor, Ludwig and Mayer, Bauer, and he did in fact bring back to England the first supplies of those new type faces that Morison delighted to display on the Gollancz publications.

The German founders had evidently not then equipped themselves to cast their types on the British and American bodies and there were some anomalies in nominating the sizes when they were laid in the Fanfare cases. The types

DIALOGUES

AND

MONOLOGUES

═══════════════════════════════

Humbert Wolfe's

first volume of

Literary Criticism

═══════════════════════════════

VICTOR GOLLANCZ

═══════════════════════════════

(84) One of the first jackets on the celebrated yellow paper.

were also cast to Didot height and had been ground down at the foot to the English height of .918″.

The jacket for *The Running Footman*, published in 1931, shows Morison at his most uninhibited and most successful exploitation of the method of approach he had developed. Here are all the tricks, the capital "L" used in a line of lower case, the word "The" set in two types to give it a sparkle and the fifteen words displayed have been broken up into seven elements all resting on the stable base of the four lines of the blurb. In some respects it has characteristics of the compositor's jobbing, with its connecting lines "by" and "author of", but what a difference in impact. In the top left hand corner McKnight Kauffer's emblem beckons like a man waving a flag, and at the foot a black fist urges us to turn the cover of the book.

Of all the types Morison used at Fanfare his favourite was the Fette Koch Antiqua, designed by Rudolf Koch for Klingspor. It was not merely because he used it more frequently but because of the way he used it, strategically, as on *The Running Footman* and monumentally on Frank Harris's *Bernard Shaw*, giving great strength to the layout. Moreover this face for all its considerable weight has great legibility, and it is not lessened by printing in colour.

To see how the Morison treatment compares with a less dynamic style see the jacket for *Dialogues and Monologues* by Humbert Wolfe, an author Gollancz knew at Benn and one of the first he published under his own imprint. Set entirely in Tiemann with great formality it gives no hint of the riot to come.

Ernest Ingham's recollections about the jackets are extremely interesting. At first the yellow paper was imported but this became expensive, and Ingham went to Spalding and Hodge and asked them to match it. With some outside help in the matter of a dye they produced a paper that satisfied everyone. When Morison found it impossible to carry on with the jackets Ingham took over. He told me that, on occasion, when Morison was not satisfied with the copy he would ask Gollancz to alter it. "I never did that," said Ingham. When he did not approve of a setting Morison would declare in a loud voice "It's lousy. Lousy."

Berthold Wolpe, the designer of that fine letter Albertus, did many of the layouts as well as Ingham. Livia Gollancz with great competence continued the manner. Miss Gollancz was no stranger to typography and has vivid memories of her father doing the layouts for his press advertisements on the dining room table at home. The main feature of these advertisements was the 12-point thick border with a jagged inside edge. This irregularity was made by compositors hacking at lead rule with a file. There was no law about the "design" of the rule, the compositors cut away until they themselves were satisfied that they had

a novel

The
RUNNING
FOOTMAN

by

JOHN OWEN

author of

'The Shepherd and the Child'

There is a certain identification of a man with the happiness and suffering of others—a sympathy natural, taken for granted, and devoid of any element of self-consciousness — the

(85) It is more instructive to the typographer to see the Gollancz jackets in black and white as it enables him to assess the structure and also to appreciate Morison's considerable power to visualise the result in print of his roughly pencilled layouts. In the original all the type was in black and the emblem that Morison commissioned from McKnight Kauffer in red.

BERNARD SHAW

BY

FRANK HARRIS

". . . This much I am obliged to say, lest it should be held that in passing the proofs for press as corrected by me I am endorsing everything that he says about me. I am **not**. But no man is a good judge of his own portrait; and if it be well painted he has no right to prevent the artist exhibiting it, or even, when the artist is a deceased friend, to refuse to varnish it before the show opens. I hope this makes my part in the matter clear.**"**

—from Bernard Shaw's Postscript

(86) The jacket for Frank Harris's "unauthorised biography" of Shaw is as commanding as a proclamation due to the carefully judged scale of heading to text. (Original: title and author in red, the rest in black on yellow.)

T*he* FIERY DIVE

STORIES BY

MARTIN ARMSTRONG

Coming after *St. Christopher's Day* (which had a unanimous success with critics and public alike) Martin Armstrong's last novel, *Sleeping Fury,* received what is known as a "mixed" reception. Its success with the public was even greater than that of *St. Christopher's Day;* but while many critics of authority considered it his finest piece of work, others of no less authority attacked it with a vigour which was itself a compliment to Martin Armstrong's artistic stature.

About the present volume of short stories there can, we think, be no such difference of opinion. Whether in the subtle psychology of the *Fiery Dive* itself, or in the remote, sun-bitten, austere atmosphere of the legendary *St. Hercules*

Continued on first flap

(87) Of "The Fiery Dive" jacket Beatrice Warde wrote that it "depends less for its exhilarating effect upon graphic shocks than upon the original and essential novelty of seeing something to be read, where one had expected to find a picture". This could well be taken as a summary of the whole concept.

(88) Opposite page. One of the occasional jackets in black and white. By accident or design it seems impossible to look at the photograph of Epstein's sculpture without at the same time taking in the studiedly simple lines of type above and below.

PAUL ROBESON
neGro

BY
Eslanda Goode Robeson

achieved the desired effect. It says much for Ingham that he gathered a staff of compositors who as cheerfully did this work as they did the fine typesetting for which Fanfare had a reputation. Later on this jagged rule was replaced by a machine-cut plain and milled combination rule, entirely losing the vibrant quality of the hand-wrought unit.

Not all the Gollancz jackets were printed on the same yellow paper. There were often occasions when it was decided to use a photograph and it was the rule to print these on cream toned matt art. One that Morison did was for Eslanda Goode Robeson's study of her husband, the celebrated negro singer Paul Robeson. The stark title of the book was *Paul Robeson negro*, and Morison set the name in Tiemann Bold capitals with the word "negro" centred underneath in lower case, except that in order to preserve the alignment, one supposes, he changed the lower case "g" to a capital. Since the size of Tiemann capital "G" that matched the x height of the "ne" and "ro" did not equal their thickness, a capital "G" of the expanded Sphinx was used instead, which though slightly thicker, roughly maintains the colour of the line. The overall simplicity of the typesetting allows Epstein's sculpture to rise out of the page. The yellow paper was from Morgan's "Radiant" series which includes an orange shade. Gollancz used this for a few jackets but although printing in black had a rich effect there was not the legibility obtained from printing on yellow paper.

In *Sailor with Banjo*, a sober touch for poetry, but still the mixture of the Caslon Old Face italic with the Baskerville giving the lyrical copy an additional lift.

In 1930 Gollancz founded a company called Mundanus Ltd., with the intention of publishing original novels in paper covers, five years before Penguin, at the then low price of three shillings, obviously considered an important sales factor because of the prominence given to it on the front cover. What Morison did with the cover for the first title, *Gunman*, is seen in the illustration. The colophon with the diminished capital "M" and the exaggerated ascender of the "d" is also by Morison. The text, in Baskerville, was well set and printed, but Mundanus did not prosper.

(89 and 90) Opposite page. A sedate wrapper for Maclaren's fanciful poetry; a busy layout for the cover of a paperback novel of the Capone era. All was grist.

8

IN PRAISE OF TIMES AND OTHER ROMANS

In his book on Morison,[1] James Moran traces the involved and important story of the Monotype Corporation's letter-cutting policy with fascinating dialectical still. Because there is no exact record of what happened when and who was responsible, and above all because human memory is a notoriously unreliable witness, it is a story from which controversy and acrimony are frequently distilled. It is an example of the soundness of the phrase "success has many fathers, failure none".[2] However it is generally agreed that Morison's contribution was not only creative but dominant, providing a stream of type faces, both newly designed ones and classical revivals; he also gave a stimulus to those who followed him at Monotype and continued the good work of preserving and adding to our typographic heritage. The book faces Morison instigated are taken for granted by publishers whose grandfathers would have had difficulty in explaining the difference between old style and modern.

Which is not at all surprising for it was not uncommon to see, in type specimen books, moderns that were called Old Face (for example, Monotype Series 137) as well as some where the onus of classification had been shirked and the type being given a number instead of a name. Bembo dominates in the best designed books of the year show; Bell, Fournier and others shine in work in that shrinking category of fine printing; the large sizes of many types are the backbone of the commercial printers' specimen books. It is often overlooked that Morison induced Gill to translate his sans serif into type, thus adding a unique design to the world's store. Gill came too late for the new typography, and in any case it did not suit the geometric ideas of that style. The instant designers of today call it "old fashioned" and so it is, having a basically humanist lower case. And it seems to me painfully obvious that the lower case letters are badly fitted, a technical fault rather than an artistic one, but which will probably never be corrected. So this creation of a master awaits a book designer who will do it justice.

"Typographer, scholar, historian of the press" ran the heading of the obituary notice of Morison in *The Times*. Its recognition of a man of many talents was appropriate, for Morison will be remembered by different people

[1] *Stanley Morison: his typographic achievement*, Lund Humphries, 1971.
[2] Coined by journalist Eric Foster.

for different reasons. The bibliophile keeps his copy of *The Tapestry* under lock and key, and the working typographer will be grateful for broadening the choice of typographic material. But these are small groups. The main group comprises the millions of ordinary readers who are the unconscious beneficiaries of his activities.

When the proprietors of *The Times* authorised Morison to design a new type face for their newspaper they had an experience similar to the man who plants a bean in his back garden and watches it grow out of sight far beyond the confines of its owner's territory. The proprietors of *The Times* may have been unprepared for what they got but Morison was by no means unprepared for the task. For years, as if in anticipation of this momentous undertaking, he had been collecting English newspapers published over the past three hundred years, studying their types, layout, editorship and paying special attention to *The Times* in the process. The results of this study took practical form in a series of six lectures in the Sandars Readership, published by Cambridge University Press in 1932. Typically Morison wrote in his introductory remarks: "Printing did not change the book. . . . In spite of the fact that printing was a new invention, it did not produce a thing which looked 'new': it was content to extend the facilities of reading (the same old scripts in the same old layouts) and writing. In a word, it miraculously increased and multiplied, and hence cheapened, books. All this is familiar to us from half-a-dozen new or old histories of printing. But we are less accustomed to reflect that the great invention of the craft is the newspaper." He had established himself as a formidable authority.

In the forty years since it was made available to all who wished to use it, Times Roman has become one of the most successful type faces of the twentieth century, in daily use all over the world, in every kind of printing and in many languages. These are simple undeniable facts which the illustrations in this section bear out.

As well as being available on all mechanical composition systems—Monotype, Linotype and Intertype—it is one of the steady sellers in the Letraset range and there is a bastardised version in the IBM computer setting called Press Roman which has been used to produce some passable printed matter.

When a new type face appears it gets the attention of the critics in the same way as does a novel, a painting or a musical composition; or, on another plane, as does a new motor car or a new fabric or building material. The tail of the "y" and the dot of the "i" are put under the microscope (literally) by the dons and dunces of the printing and literary world. But critics are known for their ability to disagree with one another and so it was with Times.

For a few years after the Times New Roman (its official name) appeared

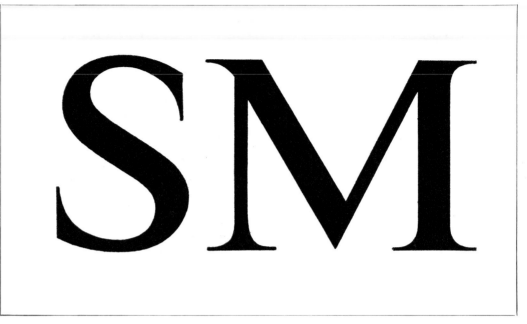

(91) These enlarged capitals of the New Times Roman reveal its classical base.

it was the fashion to say that it was not a good newspaper face but was suitable for books. When it was used for books it was said that it was only suitable for newspapers. "Not a good face, except for the plainest of factual works" wrote Garfield Howe,[1] a view which the publishing business has shown to be untrue.

But it is the fate of success to be traduced. J. B. Priestley related that when he wrote novels the critics said he should stick to the theatre and that when he wrote plays they said he should stick to being a novelist. In the same way Henry Ford suffered from critics of whom he said that whenever anyone had a success there were always people to say it would have been better if it had been different. The word for this sort of criticism is carping.

The judgement that Times was not suitable for book work is the most false of all. One has only to refer to the statistics of the National Book League's annual exhibitions to see the extent and good effect to which Times is used, and it is also a popular choice by book publishers in Europe and America. The paper-back publisher could hardly exist without it, the hundreds if not thousands of beautifully turned out Penguins that continue to be set in Times are sufficient proof of this point.

[1] *Signature*, No. 12, 1939.

The plague of frogs,   EXODUS 7, 8   *of lice, and of flies*

smite with the rod that is in mine hand upon the waters which are in the river, and they shall be turned to blood.

18 And the fish that is in the river shall die, and the river shall stink; and the Egyptians shall lothe to drink of the water of the river.

19 ¶ And the Lord spake unto Moses, Say unto Aaron, Take thy rod, and stretch out thine hand upon the waters of Egypt, upon their streams, upon their rivers, and upon their ponds, and upon all their pools of water, that they may become blood; and that there may be blood throughout all the land of Egypt, both in vessels of wood, and in vessels of stone.

20 And Moses and Aaron did so, as the Lord commanded; and he lifted up the rod, and smote the waters that were in the river, in the sight of Pharaoh, and in the sight of his servants; and all the waters that were in the river were turned to blood.

21 And the fish that was in the river died; and the river stank, and the Egyptians could not drink of the water of the river; and there was blood throughout all the land of Egypt.

22 But the magicians of Egypt did so with their enchantments: and Pharaoh's heart was hardened, neither did he hearken unto them; as the Lord had said.

23 And Pharaoh turned and went into his house, neither did he set his heart to this also.

24 And all the Egyptians digged round about the river for water to drink; for they could not drink of the water of the river.

25 And seven days were fulfilled, after that the Lord had smitten the river.

CHAPTER 8

AND the Lord spake unto Moses, Go unto Pharaoh, and say unto him, Thus saith the Lord, Let my people go, that they may serve me.

2 And if thou refuse to let them go, behold, I will smite all thy borders with frogs:

3 And the river shall bring forth frogs abundantly, which shall go up and come into thine house, and into thy bedchamber, and upon thy bed, and into the house of thy servants, and upon thy people, and into thine ovens, and into thy kneadingtroughs:

4 And the frogs shall come up both on thee, and upon thy people, and upon all thy servants.

5 ¶ And the Lord spake unto Moses, Say unto Aaron, Stretch forth thine hand with thy rod over the streams, over the rivers, and over the ponds, and cause frogs to come up upon the land of Egypt.

6 And Aaron stretched out his hand over the waters of Egypt; and the frogs came up, and covered the land of Egypt.

7 And the magicians did so with their enchantments, and brought up frogs upon the land of Egypt.

8 ¶ Then Pharaoh called for Moses and Aaron, and said, Intreat the Lord, that he may take away the frogs from me, and from my people; and I will let the people go, that they may do sacrifice unto the Lord.

9 And Moses said unto Pharaoh, Glory over me: when shall I intreat for thee, and for thy servants, and for thy people, to destroy the frogs from thee and thy houses, that they may remain in the river only?

10 And he said, To morrow. And he said, Be it according to thy word: that thou mayest know that there is none like unto the Lord our God.

11 And the frogs shall depart from thee, and from thy houses, and from thy servants, and from thy people; they shall remain in the river only.

12 And Moses and Aaron went out from Pharaoh: and Moses cried unto the Lord because of the frogs which he had brought against Pharaoh.

13 And the Lord did according to the word of Moses; and the frogs died out of the houses, out of the villages, and out of the fields.

14 And they gathered them together upon heaps: and the land stank.

15 But when Pharaoh saw that there was respite, he hardened his heart, and hearkened not unto them; as the Lord had said.

16 ¶ And the Lord said unto Moses, Say unto Aaron, Stretch out thy rod, and smite the dust of the land, that it may become lice throughout all the land of Egypt.

17 And they did so; for Aaron stretched out his hand with his rod, and smote the dust of the earth, and it became lice in man, and in beast; all the dust of the land became lice throughout all the land of Egypt.

18 And the magicians did so with their enchantments to bring forth lice, but they could not: so there were lice upon man, and upon beast.

19 Then the magicians said unto Pharaoh, This is the finger of God: and Pharaoh's heart was hardened, and he hearkened not unto them; as the Lord had said.

20 ¶ And the Lord said unto Moses, Rise up early in the morning, and stand before Pharaoh; lo, he cometh forth to the water; and say unto him, Thus saith the Lord, Let my people go, that they may serve me.

21 Else, if thou wilt not let my people go, behold, I will send swarms of flies upon thee, and upon thy servants, and upon thy people, and into thy houses: and the houses of the Egyptians shall be full of swarms of flies, and also the ground whereon they are.

22 And I will sever in that day the land of Goshen, in which my people dwell, that no swarms of flies shall be there; to the end thou mayest know that I am the Lord in the midst of the earth.

23 And I will put a division between my people and thy people: to morrow shall this sign be.

24 And the Lord did so; and there came a grievous swarm of flies into the house of Pharaoh, and into his servants' houses, and

47

(92) To be deemed good enough for a bible by Cambridge University Press sets the seal on Times as a book face. This is a page from the popular Cambridge Pitt octavo bible set in Times semi-bold series 421, an adaptation over which Morison took enormous trouble.

ELIZABETH II

Trade Descriptions Act 1972

1972 CHAPTER 34

An Act to require certain names and marks applied to imported goods to be accompanied by an indication of origin. [29th June 1972]

BE IT ENACTED by the Queen's most Excellent Majesty, by and with the advice and consent of the Lords Spiritual and Temporal, and Commons, in this present Parliament assembled, and by the authority of the same, as follows:—

1.—(1) Where a name or mark which—

    (*a*) is a United Kingdom name or mark; or

    (*b*) is likely to be taken for a United Kingdom name or mark (whether or not such a United Kingdom name or mark actually exists);

Indication of origin on certain imported goods.

is applied to goods manufactured or produced outside the United Kingdom, subsection (2) of this section shall apply except as otherwise provided by or under this section.

(2) If any person, in the course of a trade or business, supplies or offers to supply the goods, then, unless—

    (*a*) the name or mark is accompanied by a conspicuous indication of the country in which the goods were manufactured or produced; or

    (*b*) the name or mark is neither visible in the state in which the goods are supplied or offered nor likely to become visible on such inspection as may reasonably be expected to be made of the goods by a person to whom they are to be supplied;

the person supplying or offering to supply the goods shall, subject to the provisions of this Act, be guilty of an offence.

(93) The Stationery Office sets a high standard for its mundane printing and is a consistent user of Times.

ОТ ПЕРЕВОДЧИКА

Так как английские имена обыкновенно передаются по-русски звукоподражательно, а не орфографически, мы пытались помочь русскому читателю, несколько улучшив традиционный русский метод. Это касается главным образом английских букв H и W, хотя иногда наше пользование также буквой «З» вместо конечной буквы «С» может оказаться незнакомым русскому читателю.

1. Английская буква «H», которая в течение столетий заменялась русской буквой «Г», здесь была заменена буквой «Х», которая, если ее произнести легко, очень близка правильному английскому произношению. Таким образом мы писали «Hamlet» как «Хамлет», а не «Гамлет», что английскому уху звучит совершенно неправильно. Мы, впрочем, иногда уступали русской традиции в тех случаях, когда имя известно русским в старой форме, напр. «Гораций» для имени «Horace». В этом отношении нас радовал метод, усвоенный журналом «Иностранная литература», который заменяет англ. букву «H» русской буквой «Х».

2. Английская буква «W», за которой следует гласная, здесь передавалась русской буквой «у», вопреки русской практике писать ее через русское «В», что правильно для немецкой буквы «W», но в действительности не передает английской буквы «W», и в придачу смешивает ее с антл. буквой «V».

Translator's Note

Since English names are traditionally rendered in Russian by transcribing the pronunciation and not the spelling, we have tried to assist the Russian reader by slightly improving on the traditional Russian method. The chief letters involved are the English H and W, although our use also of 3 for the final S may sometimes be unfamiliar to Russian readers.

1. The English H, which Russians have for centuries transcribed as Г, has here been represented by the Russian X, which if pronounced lightly is very near to the correct English pronunciation. We have thus written Hamlet as Хамлет and not Гамлет which to the English ear sounds quite wrong. We have, however, occasionally yielded to the Russian tradition where a name is only recognizable to a Russian in the older form, e.g. Гораций for Horace. We have been encouraged by the fact that the journal 'Innostrannaya Literatura' now transcribes the English H as X.

2. The English W followed by a vowel has been rendered here by the Russian У, contrary to the Russian practice of using the Cyrillic B, which is correct for the German W, but does not truly represent the English W, and in addition causes confusion with the English V; e.g. Darwin should be Даруин and not Дарвин.

3. The final S on the end of some English names, such as Charles, James, has here been correctly transcribed by the Russian 3, and not by С e.g. Уарлз, Джеимз.

4. It is impossible to transcribe the

Modern commercial considerations demand that a type face be extrapolated to a family. The basic design must be adapted to light, bold, condensed, elongated and expanded versions and then to extra light, extra bold and extra condensed. Sometimes the drawing office (for by this time the designer has usually fled) is pressed to make italic versions for some of these permutations. Fortunately Times has been spared this extreme exploitation, and the development of the series has been done with great good judgement as a glance at the printed matter of everyday life amply demonstrates. Now that it is no longer used in *The Times* newspaper itself it seems to me that there is a perfect opportunity to honour its creator by magnanimously following an established precedent and renaming it Morison Roman.

ΑΒΓΔΕΖΗΘΙ

ΚΛΜΝΞΟ

ΠΡΣΤΥ

ΦΧΨ

Ω

(95) Greek, but unmistakably Times.

9

MORISON AND THE MODERN MOVEMENT

In the very same year that Morison started work at the Pelican Press, Professor Walter Gropius merged two schools in Weimar, Germany—the Arts and Crafts and The Academy—to become the legendary Bauhaus Institute. Historical coincidence of this sort is merely coincidence but it offers an opportunity for interesting speculation, such as what would have happened to type design and book production in England if Morison had lent his great talent to the development of a new rather than the preservation of a traditional style.

It is worthwhile remembering that the Bauhaus was not primarily concerned with typography and the fact that it is often presumed that this was so is due more than anything else to the energy and creative power of one of the most enthusiastic propagandists for the Institute's ideas, Jan Tschichold, a teacher of lettering at the School of Printing in Leipzig.

The New Typography, as it was called, caught on and rapidly spread all over continental Europe though less pervadingly in England and the United States. Its greatest success was among designers working in advertising but in book work it made little headway.

Morison was "antipathetic to the sort of rethinking of the designer's function that went on at the Bauhaus" wrote Joseph Rykwert,[1] Professor of Art at the University of Essex, and with the benefit of hindsight Morison made his attitude plain in *The Typographic Book*:

Recent years, that is after the 1914–18 war, have witnessed an increasing tendency in England and elsewhere to reject the influence of classical and historical styles and the art of the private presses, and, indeed, all conventional forms. Although this tendency is most pronounced in non-literary application a number of books have been printed in what can only be described as an "anti-art" style. The reaction against "art" in typography began in Germany. It fought for a functional solution to all problems of design. The movement grew out of Morris's protest in the

[1] In a letter to the author.

seventies against Victorian vulgarity, and dishonesty in art, but as trans-
lated in continental terms, it took a course opposite to that initiated by
the English Arts and Crafts Society.

The problem is the problem of all style: to develop a pattern which is at
once within the conventions, recognisable as the work of one man or office,
and yet sufficiently elastic to avoid monotony.

If it must be admitted that the style of much of the "fine" printing
achieved in England and America from Pickering and Morris to Updike
and Rogers is anachronistic, it may be that this period of eclectic revolution was necessary if knowledge of the right, that is the truly rational, way
to print was to be found. In printing, and perhaps in other arts, it is healthy
if not necessary, to look back to the basic principles which underlie the
work of the old masters. If it is against the highest interests of typography
to step back to Garamond, Aldus, Jenson and the period usages thereof,
the forward step may not necessarily be to remove serifs, abolish capitals,
reduce punctuation, revise spelling, and reverse margins.

Hasty acceptance, as authoritative of present architectural styles and the
elaboration of typographical mannerisms derived from them, is no more
healthy for the art of typography that the slavish imitation of any styles
of the past.

In a lecture to the College of Art at Edinburgh in 1944 he went further,
asserting that the Bauhaus was "more intellectual than rational" and whatever
that means it is certain that Morison meant it disparagingly. He went on to
say "the sanction of public opinion was not forthcoming" and it was "doubt-
ful if confidence in a new style developed between the wars will be forthcoming", and it was "wiser to regard the Bauhaus period as already at an
end."

Morison was of course a traditionalist and there is little in his work that
cannot be found in classical book work. Better typecasting, more regularity
(monotonous regularity some think) in machine-made paper than that
made by hand, a different technique of printing where the aim is to let the
type "kiss" the paper rather than press itself into it, may help to give a more
accomplished overall look to a book but there is no greater virtuosity in its
typography. Morison could justify his preference for he had the essential
inventiveness, his style was as he put it "sufficiently elastic to avoid monotony". I find it easy to accept his choice. There was to his eye a devastating
sameness about modern typography, and there was a warmth about serif
types totally absent in those types from which they had been removed.

Nevertheless the modern movement cannot and must not be suppressed indefinitely. Now, half a century after it really began typographers in America and notably in France are beginning to produce books free of traditional concepts of design. Their work is admired in England, and it is only a matter of time before it happens here.

APPENDIX

Some personal recollections

My first acquaintance with Stanley Morison was through his writings and the sight of various examples of his work from the Pelican Press and elsewhere. About this time, the early nineteen-twenties, I was a student at the L.C.C.'s Central School of Arts and Crafts in Southampton Row under the austere eye of J. H. Mason, some of whose utterances made a permanent impression on me no less than did Morison's though the two together tended to be a little unsettling.

"Typography," declared Mason to me in oracular tones, "is making black marks on white paper." Yet there was Morison with a weakness for toned paper and certainly not averse to printing type in colour.

"Type is so decorative in itself that it has no need of ornament," Mason said, and he permitted only the occasional use of the exuberant italic swash capitals of Caslon Old Face but nothing more. So what was I to think about the flower revival?

"I have only one aim, to produce magnificent words in magnificent format"; this was an area in which both men would have been in complete agreement, although at that time Morison had not done a great deal of fine bookwork.

As to advertising Mason's view was that it was not only wasteful generally but often quite useless. "All that is necessary is a classification of resources."

Mason was first and last a teacher even though, like Morison, he entered printing by accident. Morison, though he took no practical part and showed little interest in technical training, was nevertheless a great educator. To read any article or book by him was to become drawn into the net of typography or one of its many aspects; by practical example he improved the taste of many people engaged in book production, thereby benefitting countless thousands of readers.

Mason and Morison must have met if only at the offices of *The Imprint*, but they appear to have made little impact on one another, surprising at least as far as Morison was concerned for he usually had something to say about notabilities in the trade. He admired many people and said so. Of those for whom he felt some antipathy there was the rough side of his tongue. His comments were sometimes not only undeserved but inaccurate. For example, Charles Jacobi of The Chiswick Press was helpful to him at Burns and Oates, but Morison described him as "the greatest bore in Christendom and very ignorant".[1] And he referred to Bernard Newdigate as "old Newdigate" in a tasteless play on his name. It happened that both these men were physically unimposing, and Newdigate had in addition a high pitched voice, the opposite of the dominating Morison. Jacobi, described by Harry Batsford[2] as a "dapper, alert little man, black-bearded and waxed-moustached", was also in marked contrast to the unconventional, sometimes slightly unkempt Morison.

Newdigate's reputation is established, and Jacobi was not only a good printer but wrote a number of books about book production setting out sound principles. He was interested in the trade, and when asked in 1901 what he thought would improve the standard of print he made the following far-sighted comment:

> One very simple suggestion I would make for the betterment of printing as an art would be: given the opportunity, let the apprentice or workman take a greater and more intelligent interest in the work of his department. If this were generally so, I am sure it would be an all-round improvement. This reflection does not apply to all, but it does to a large proportion, largely owing to competition, and its resulting sub-division of labour is one reason for this lack of interest.[3]

For many years I regularly met John Tarr who was head of the drawing office at Monotype and in close touch with Morison. From Tarr I got many anecdotes about Morison, one of which concerning Bertram Evans I recounted to James Moran who printed it in his book *Stanley Morison: his typographic achievement*. Evans said of Morison that "he wrote books about books in museums and the books he wrote went back into museums". It happened that Evans was having some specimen pages set for a magazine, *Printing Review*, of which he was then the editor, and on looking at them Morison failed to recognise the type face. "Couldn't recognise his own Baskerville" crowed the diminutive Bertram, pleased to score off the man who meanly said of him that he looked like a squashed toad. During a visit to Tarr at his home I was made aware of another aspect of Morison's character. Tarr was showing me a number of delightful examples of printing from America, and I asked him how he had got hold of them. He said that Morison had given them to him, adding that he was a very generous man.

[1] *Stanley Morison*, Nicolas Barker. (Macmillan.)
[2] *A Batsford Century*. (Batsford.)
[3] *Caxton Magazine*, April, 1901.

But Morison is not the only one to fail to identify a type face (or a quotation) correctly; it happens all the time. In a Nonesuch booklet, *Prospect and Retrospect*, a type face was wrongly named, and I pointed this out to Francis Meynell who replied haughtily that he would rather be guilty of a thousand errors of typography than one of bad manners. Again, in 1937 I wrote an article in which I used a sentence from Dibdin for a specimen setting and Meynell wrote to me asking where the quotation came from, saying that he thought it was a "modern fake antique". I am sure Morison would have recognised Dibdin.

I well remember one morning during 1928 when Morison appeared unexpectedly in the composing room of the Fanfare Press. It was fairly early, and Ingham had not yet arrived and the overseer was elsewhere. Since someone had to acknowledge him, being nearest I went up to him, told him my name and asked if I could be of any help. It was not the first time I had seen him but at close quarters I was aware of a tall man, cold and almost aloof, with a serious expression, looking down at me in more senses than one. I was slightly taken aback, not being a great respecter of persons, and in any case I believed Morison depended on compositors and was undoubtedly helped by them whether he realised it or not. Certainly he owed something to Ingham for the trouble he took to find his craftsmen, but I never knew any one of them who could recall an occasion when they felt any kinship with Morison.

An encounter of another kind happened some twenty years later when I sent a 3-inch single column advertisement to *The Times Literary Supplement*. It announced a new book by Immanuel Velikovsky and to get the name Velikovsky as big as possible I wanted it set vertically. I had a telephone call from Derry, the advertisement manager, asking me if the layout could be altered, with the line set horizontally in the normal way, because Morison thought it might offend the paper's rather conservative-minded readers. I asked Derry to remind Morison of the occasion in 1928 when he had set a line of type vertically on the cover of a programme for the Federation of Master Printers and defended it on the grounds that it was attention-getting; my reason was the same. Whether Derry did so or not I don't know but I heard no more about it and the advertisement duly appeared as I wanted it.

A more harmonious occasion on which I was brought in touch with Morison was when I was asked by the advertising agency, Rumble Crowther and Nicholas, to do the layout of the *Times Motoring Supplement*, a review of the motor show held in the autumn of 1949. I did this and also planned the photograph used on the cover which showed Denham village reflected in the wheel disc of a Hillman Minx. I was told that the job had to be approved by

Morison and when the proofs were presented to him he made only one modification, adding a swollen rule to the contents page.

In the summer of 1953 Morison wrote to me at Sidgwick and Jackson asking if I could find him a copy of *The Battle of Nieuport* published in facsimile by the Shakespeare Association with which the firm had some connection. After some fairly tiresome letter-writing, telephoning and footwork I found a small quantity of the books in the basement of a bookseller in the Strand. I purchased a copy and walked up to Fetter Lane and delivered it personally to Morison. "How much do I owe you?" he asked, obviously pleased, and produced the few shillings from his pocket. Later that year he wrote again, mentioning *Catherine*, the book of poems by R. C. K. Ensor ("now historic" he reminded me) which was published by Sidgwicks in 1924, being the first book to be set in the newly-cast Garamond type. He wondered if a copy of a leaflet he wrote about the type had survived. I sent him a copy of the leaflet which had been sent out with the book but he disowned it. "From the look of it" he wrote, "I opine that it was written by Sidgwick himself, doubtless on the basis of some material I gave him," thus adding another thread to the complicated Garamond story.

These are all quite trivial occasions, and I have never had any dealings with Morison on matters of great importance. However, during the past fifty years I have read a great deal of his writings and seen much of the printing in which he had a hand, and I have the sense of being on familiar ground in any discussion about him. The closest I ever came to understanding him was not by personal contact but by studying the scrapbook he compiled mostly during the nineteen-twenties. It has a home-made look, a hundred sheets of thick cartridge paper stabbed together at the spine and covered with a rather crude patterned paper. Roughly pasted on the pages in no particular order are a hundred or so examples of all kinds of typography: pages from catalogues of books, prospectuses, advertisements, invitations, specimens of type faces, items designed by Bruce Rogers, F. W. Goudy and others whom he admired; envelopes addressed to him in distinguished hands from various parts of the world; a letter from Victor Gollancz which starts: "My dear Morison, here is the copy for the jackets . . . ." Then amidst all this fascinating material he has pasted down the humblest example of printing he could find—the outer wrapper, with the original black and green design, of a packet of Wild Woodbine cigarettes. It is the gesture of a man who had a totally absorbing interest in all printed things.

INDEX

THE END